Walk – Don't Run

A Childhood Memoir

By Scott Paulson

Copyright © 2022 Scott F. Paulson

All rights reserved. No portion of this book may be used or reproduced by any means, graphic, electronic or mechanical, including photocopying, recording, taping, or by any information storage retrieval system, without the written permission of the publisher except in the case of brief quotations embodied in critical articles or reviews.

Dedication

To my parents, Fred and Ronelva, my sister Sue, and my brother Brett.

Disclaimer: This book reflects my recollection of events from my past. To the best of my recollection, these events occurred in 1960. An effort has been made to keep historical incidents accurate for educational purposes. Dialogue has been recreated from my memory. There is no intent to harm any persons in the memoir.

The final edit of this book was completed on May 14, 2025.

The cover photo is the house at 2500 North Raynor Avenue in Crest Hill, Illinois, where the Fred Paulson family lived in 1960.

Table of Contents

Introduction 5

Chapter One: The Summer Ends 6

Chapter Two: The First Day of School 12

Chapter Three: Riverview Amusement Park 24

Chapter Four: Activities 40

Chapter Five: Sundays...54

Chapter Six: The End of the First Grading Period...................................59

Chapter Seven: Playing by Ear 65

Chapter Eight: Halloween 71

Chapter Nine: Murph...80

Chapter Ten: Guilty...89

Chapter Eleven: John F. Kennedy..101

Chapter Twelve: Politics and Prejudices 114

Chapter Thirteen: Fooling the Class Bully 128

Chapter Fourteen: Anticipating Christmas 134

Chapter Fifteen: Christmas 138

Chapter Sixteen: New Year's Eve 149

Chapter Seventeen: Fast Forward 165

About the Author...168

Introduction

"Walk – Don't Run" is a memoir detailing my life's adventures as a 10-year-old boy growing up in the Midwest American city of Joliet, Illinois, in 1960. Though just a child, I was pushed into young adulthood in a number of ways. The first-time experiences encountered during that time ranged from the joys of finding success in my musical prowess to the confusing sadness endured when my grandfather passed away. It was the first time I experienced a death in the family. I brought on some of my burdens myself as I was a serious child much of the time. I admittedly worried about too many things going on in my life of which I had no control.

My family, which consisted of my mom, dad, older sister, and younger brother, consumed me. In addition, my small circle of close friends, my school life including its many extracurricular activities, my church life, and my growing love of music had tremendous influences on me. The busy life was a lot for me, as a young boy, to endure. However, I knew I had to do my best to succeed for my mother, who wanted and demanded what she believed was best for me, as well as for my father, who was the one person I would never want to disappoint. The names of some people in this memoir have been changed.

Chapter One: The Summer Ends

I could never understand why some kids looked so forward to the first day of school at the end of each summer vacation. To me, the beginning of a new school year meant the end of swimming almost every day at the neighborhood pool and having practically no more free time. Days with bad weather when the pool was closed and the week I was away from home on our family's annual vacation were the only days I didn't get to the swimming pool. My only obligations during the summer were being at the dinner table at five o'clock in the afternoon when Dad got home from work, getting dressed up to go to church on Sunday, and getting to my music lessons on time once a week.

The thing I disliked most about school starting again was that I had to get up so early in the morning. School starting meant I would have to start getting up before 7 o'clock in the morning again. In the summer, I would usually sleep until eight o'clock or even later. I never knew why one hour made such a big difference to me, but it did. This past summer, unfortunately, Mom got my sister Sue, my little brother Brett, and me up a little before eight o'clock many days. Mom got us up and fed us breakfast early because she started walking to Grandma's house by eight o'clock almost every day since early July of that summer. Because Brett was so young, just five years old, she took him with her on the half-hour walk.

Ever since Grandpa died in early July of the past summer, Mom spent more time at Grandma's house than at home during the day. When I overheard Mom talking to someone about Grandpa's death, she said something about him taking Grandma shopping in their car in downtown Joliet. She said that Grandpa always stayed in the car because he didn't like shopping. On the early July afternoon when he died, he had stayed in the hot car and the heat apparently killed him. Anyway, even though Grandma must have needed my mom more than we needed her at home, I wanted Mom home with us for the summer. Summer just wasn't the same without having Mom around all the time. I thought it would have been nice if Dad had taken some time off work to do summer things with us. However, that never happened because he had to work every Monday through Friday. It was selfish of me, and I felt guilty about it. However, the feeling of wanting Mom at home lasted right up until the end of the summer. I was never rude enough to put it in words to anyone, but I'm sure my occasional long face showed how unhappy I was about the summer of 1960 at our house.

More than that, I was disappointed in myself through the family ordeal. I felt like there should have been a time when I would cry after Grandpa died. Isn't that what a person does when someone in the family dies? Even though I felt very bad about Grandpa dying, I couldn't cry about it. I felt more like crying for Grandma because she now had to live without Grandpa. They were always together like two best friends. When concentrating on that still couldn't make me cry, I kept myself awake one night in bed and thought about how sad Mom must have been. After all, it was her dad who died. Still, I couldn't cry. I couldn't understand how I could have something so sad happen, yet I couldn't cry about it. Maybe I would have been sadder and have been able to cry if Mom and Dad had let us kids go to the wake or funeral. However, on the evening of Grandpa's wake, Mom walked us over to a neighbor's front yard and told us to stay there until she and Dad would get home. When I asked why I couldn't go, she said I was too young for this and said that I wouldn't want to go since they would be staying late. Though I really did not want to see Grandpa dead, out of sheer curiosity I wanted to see what was going on. I was anxious to see how Grandma was doing, too. I was worried about her but afraid to ask my mom how she was doing. I didn't want to know if she wasn't doing well since I couldn't do anything to help her at the time.

As we stayed with the neighbors, we were in front of their house with the kids in that family. After it got dark, the fireworks started as they were on display every year on the night before July 4th, Independence Day. Out of all of us kids, Brett was most impressed with the long and powerful fireworks display. I played a trick on him and told him that these fireworks were for his birthday, which would be in a couple of days. He actually believed me. He sat there watching the rest of the fireworks display with his smug nose up in the air and smirking as if he was really special. Sue and the neighborhood kids helped me out by also saying that all these fireworks lighting up the sky and making all that noise was for his birthday. I'm not sure how many years he thought those fireworks were in honor of his birthday, but it lasted for a couple of years. Every year, we got a big kick out of his naivety.

By the end of this particular summer, I disliked the thought of going back to school more than ever because I had felt as though this summer wasn't good enough. I wished I could have been more like Sue and her friends. They were always so excited to go back to school. Not only was I awkward about not wanting to go back to school, but I couldn't even cry about Grandpa dying. I felt I wasn't like other people at all. On one hand, I figured that there must have been something terribly wrong with me, but I had no idea what it was. On the other hand, maybe the only thing that was wrong with me was that I worried too much about myself. After all, nobody else treated me as if I was very different. Yet, I felt I was different from others. Even though I tried not thinking about it too often, I did. At the age of ten, thinking I was different from others was a huge concern to me. I wondered if I would always be different from other people.

In spite of having to get up early and having to lose my free time when school would start, there were a couple of things I liked about school starting again. The couple of things I looked forward to each September were things of personal interest to me. I liked the suspense of finding out who my new teacher would be. Having a sister who was two years older than I was, I had already heard about the teachers. This year, I had heard much about all of the fifth-grade teachers from Sue and other kids since all of those teachers had taught at Chaney Public Grade School for a long, long time. From what I had heard, it didn't matter which teacher I would get for fifth grade since all three of the teachers sounded like they were about the same. They were all older than my mom but younger than my grandmother. While that wasn't bad, I didn't like hearing that all of them give lots of homework.

I also liked finding out which kids would be in my class and who would end up sitting near me. I liked some kids at the school, and I would enjoy getting to know them better. Obviously, these were the ones I would want seated near me. Then there were kids I had wished would have moved over the summer, but they wouldn't move anywhere. I wouldn't want them in my classroom. If they ended up in my class, I wouldn't want them sitting near me. However, if they changed over the summer by becoming nicer, maybe I would start liking them.

Being somewhat shy, I only had a few friends at school, but the friends I had were good friends. Our school was small enough for just about everybody to know everyone's faces, but it was too big for everybody to know everyone's name. The school had three fifth grade classrooms with about 30 students in each class. Most kids seemed to be part of a big group of friends. That may have only been what I thought, though. I wasn't in one of those big groups and often felt left out because of it. However, with the few good friends I had, I convinced myself that I didn't stick out and appear as awkward as a few kids who had no friends at all. I never wanted to be one of those kids who had no friends. Being friendless would have been very tough for me. Beyond lonely, it would have made me feel more unusual than I already felt.

The only other thing I liked about going back to school each year was getting my new books. Actually, the books were never brand new ones, but they were books that weren't mine before. Getting textbooks that were more difficult to read was always a thrill because it reminded me that I was getting older. Anything that reminded me that I was a little closer to being an adult made me feel good. Unlike many kids, I was serious most of the time. People like me should have been born at the age of twenty or older, I guess. I rarely felt like the kid I was. The only childish trait I ever saw in me was my fear of being alone in the dark when I was alone in the basement of our family's house. Yet, fearing the dark at times may be something that frightens some adults, too. Anyway, being young, I had to go to school. Receiving new books was one of the joys in it for me.

Each year when I received the new textbooks from the teacher, I stacked them in the order of my fondness of the subject. My two favorite subjects, math and reading, were about tied. I put the math book on top of the pile. Math won out because I was very good at it. Unless my math homework involved tricky story problems, it took me the least amount of time to finish. Working with numbers, to me, was also like doing a puzzle or a game. I enjoyed doing it most of the time. My reading book would be next, followed by my writing tablet. The history book, followed by the science book, was next. Finally, I would put the drawing tablet on the bottom of the pile. I didn't like drawing or doing artwork. Of course, that made me feel awkward, too, because it seemed like everybody else loved to draw and do artwork. For some strange reason, I never worked well with crayons, colored pencils, glue, scissors, and other supplies needed for art class. When I was instructed to draw something or create something with art supplies, it wasn't pretty, to say the least.

Almost every year, as I recall, we had to write about our summer vacation during the first day of school when I was in grade school. No doubt, I would be writing that essay again for the fifth-grade teacher as soon as school would start. Our school had classes from kindergarten to eighth grade, and some called it an elementary school while most people called it a grade school back then. That first writing assignment was so predictable. I would hate being told to write about my summer again. I already had the outline for the assignment in my head since I had done it several times before on the first day of school in the past. I was determined to write it quickly so that I could start snooping through my new books when I had completed writing it. I would write about going swimming at the pool down the street, going to my music lessons once a week, and tell where my family went on our summer vacation. I wouldn't bother with all of the summer vacation's details because I thought the teacher wouldn't read the paper very thoroughly anyway. As far as writing the negatives about the summer, including the death of my grandfather, I didn't want to write about it. Teachers were so busy on the first day of school that I figured they just tried to keep their students busy doing something while they were busy getting their classroom chores done. The first writing assignment wouldn't be a problem for me as I was a good writer for a kid, according to my mom and my previous teachers. Therefore, I knew I didn't need to put a whole lot of effort into this assignment. Hopefully, the fifth-grade teacher would think I was a good writer, too, after eventually taking time to read my various writing assignments.

Chapter Two: The First Day of School

The first day of the 1960-1961 school year arrived. As Mom got me up a little before 7 o'clock, the first thing I thought about was that I was exactly half of the way through Chaney Public Grade School. It went up to eighth grade. Therefore, having been promoted four times, I would have to be promoted another four times before I would graduate from there and go to high school. I hoped the last half would go by much faster than the first half did. Incidentally, I never went to kindergarten because the school couldn't afford it the year I was five years old. So, I was exactly in the middle of my eight years at this school. I had four down and four to go.

Anyway, I washed up in the bathroom. Then I ate two pieces of French toast with lots of melted butter on them, as I didn't like maple syrup back then, and drank a glass of milk. As a matter of fact, I didn't like French toast either, but drowning it in butter made it edible for me. Mom always had breakfast waiting for me on the kitchen table shortly after 7 o'clock. After eating, I went to the bathroom to wash up again and brushed my teeth. The mornings my sister was in there, I would usually forget about washing up and brushing my teeth. Then I got out of my pajamas, and got into my new school clothes. As I knew it would be, my shirt was stiff. My jeans were stiff, too. My new shoes were also uncomfortably stiff. These stiff clothes added to my unhappiness about the first day of school. If it were my choice, I would only have worn clothes I had worn before. They would be comfortable because I would have already broken them in. New clothes, by the way, made a person stand out in a crowd, too. Due to the clothes Mom had bought me, I would stand out a lot. Shy people like me don't like to stand out in crowds, and I was just about the shyest person I ever knew. The shirt Mom had summoned me to wear on the first day of fifth grade had little black circular designs on a blue background. I thought it was hideous. However, being dark colors, it was only somewhat noticeable. I knew better than to argue about wearing it since I had argued about having to wear new clothes that Mom had chosen for me in the past, and I didn't get very far with my objections. She had a way of making me feel guilty for criticizing. She told me that if clothes were new, they cost lots of money and I should appreciate them. Complaining, when I should be thankful, was apparently no less than sinful.

By 7:15, I was usually ready to go to school. Yes, I was a fast eater, especially when I was anxious about getting to school on time. Yet, I would probably have to wait at least another 15 minutes or so for Sue to finish getting ready to go to school. As I waited for Sue to come out of the bathroom, I watched cartoons on television. My sister never stopped amazing me with her morning routine. She would get out of bed with big pink rollers in her hair. By the time we would leave for school, she would transform herself from a creature that fit my image of a Martian to a pretty seventh grade girl. I never saw her take time to eat breakfast either. She was remarkable. Even though I resented having to wait for her every school morning, I felt extremely lucky that I could get ready in such a short amount of time. The big difference was probably our hair. I didn't even have to comb my crew cut.

Even though I'm referring to my sister by the name Sue, which is the name most people called her most of the time, she was called a variety of other names in our family. Mom usually called her Susie. Besides calling her Sue, Dad sometimes called her Sue-Sue or Sues. I usually followed Dad's lead and called her Sue most of the time, but sometimes I called her Sue-Sue. Grandma and other family members usually called her by her proper name, Susan. Five-year-old Brett called her any one of the names that the rest of us used which were Sue, Susie, Susan, Sues, and Sue-Sue. Though I'm not sure, he probably picked the name he had last heard used to identify her. I don't think she minded going by all of the names that she was called because I never heard her complain about it.

I never let my sister know that waiting for her in the morning aggravated me. If she had known, she would probably have told me to go ahead without her. However, I was more comfortable when I walked with her rather than walking alone. I really liked being with her a lot. Besides being very pretty, she was very popular. I was always proud to be seen with her and to let people know that she was my sister. Also, by being in different grades, I didn't get much of a chance to see her or to talk to her during the school day. Though we were both in the school band and had band rehearsal together from eight o'clock until nine o'clock in the morning, I wouldn't see her the rest of the school day. At least I had a chance to talk to her during the 15-minute morning walk to band practice that we had for one hour before school started every school day.

On this first day of the new school year, my sister was finally ready to leave just as Mom was getting Brett up. We wished him lots of luck since it was a big day for him. It was his first day of kindergarten. The school assigned Brett to the morning session, which meant he would be in school for about three hours in the morning, starting at nine o'clock. That would be all. Therefore, Mom would walk him to school around 8:30 and have to walk back to school in a few hours to walk him home. Sue and I would be in school until about three o'clock. Because of the hour-long band rehearsal in the morning, we had a longer day than most of the students.

As Sue and I walked through the living room to head to school, we grabbed our music folders, new school supplies, and lunch boxes as we ate lunch at school most days rather than come home during the lunch hour. After all, we would have to spend half of the lunchtime walking since it took about 15 minutes for the walk each way. As we had in the past when school was in session, we began the seven-block walk east on Rose Avenue to school. It was unusual to see the sun so low in the sky again. During the summer, I didn't get outside this early to see the sun there. It would almost be directly overhead by the time I would head for the swimming pool after eating lunch during the summer. On this first day of school, after we had walked about two blocks, Sue gasped, "My clarinet!" While she stood there with our things on the ground, I ran back to the house, found her clarinet case in the living room closet, wiped the dust off of it by rubbing it against the stomach area of my shirt, and ran back to continue the long walk to school. Mom didn't even seem to notice that I came back as she was probably having breakfast with Brett in the kitchen before getting him ready for his first day of kindergarten.

It was precisely seven-and-a-half blocks from our front door to the school's gym door where we would enter for band rehearsal. We usually walked in sometime between 8:02 and 8:05, a little late. When we got to the gym door, I blocked the door with an outstretched arm, and I told Sue to put her things down on the ground so she would have free fingers to scratch my back. The stiffness of the new shirt was causing my back to be terribly itchy. From experience, I knew I couldn't reach enough of my back with my own two hands to do the job, and I didn't want to walk into the band rehearsal while desperately needing my back scratched.

First of all, we would already be noticeable from walking in late. Scratching myself in my new clothes would only make me even more noticeable. After all, God had already made me a very noticeable person, as I was one of the tallest kids my age and one of the chubbiest kids in the school, so I thought. It appeared to me that other tall kids were skinny and other chubby kids were short. I was the only kid I knew who was both tall and chubby. Therefore, I did not need new, weird-looking clothes that I would constantly be scratching to make me stand out even more.

My sister scratched my back harder than usual, likely due to her dissatisfaction in having to help me when we were already running late on the first day. Then we walked into the huge gymnasium, saw the band set up at the far end of the gym as it had been in the past, and quickly tiptoed across the hard wood floor so we wouldn't make too much noise in our new school shoes. Sue seemed to tiptoe much better than I was able to do. My shoes occasionally made a sound that echoed throughout the otherwise quiet gym. We took our seats while Mr. Mattei stood patiently on his podium. Every time he had to wait for us, he would hold his baton in his clasped hands in front of his big belly, and he would try not to scowl. On this first day, however, he didn't even look irritated. His facial expression showed that he was glad to see us back in band for another year. Before he continued talking to the band students in front of him, he instructed me, "Wet your reed." I thought that all the students were watching us prepare for rehearsal. I hated the unwanted attention. Even though I wanted to rub my back against the back of my chair to sooth the returning itchiness, I didn't since I felt that some band members were still looking my way. However, I may have just been shyly paranoid. I don't know.

Walking into band rehearsal late was something I don't think I ever could have done alone. I was able to do it with Sue at my side, though. I sat in the first row, and she sat in the third row. She was more popular than I was by a long shot, but I was the better musician. I think she was in the band because her friends were in it while I was in the band because I loved to make music.

During the past two school years when I was in third and fourth grades, older kids may have thought it was funny to see a younger guy like me sit up in the first row with older kids in the clarinet section. However, for the first time, during this first band practice in fifth grade, I sensed resentment from a couple of the older girls who sat around me. No one said a word to me. They just leaned away so I wouldn't touch them when I sat down. Other years, these older kids lightly poked me in the side or did something to make me feel welcome when I would get to rehearsal. They had often asked me, "How's your sister doing today, Scott?" However, they were saying nothing to me so far this year. To them, I guess I wasn't a cute little kid anymore. Honestly, I never thought I was. According to their attitudes, I was now older and should have known my place. I'm certain that my place, according to them, was somewhere, anywhere, behind the first row. But I was in that first row to stay. Furthermore, I had my eye on the first chair in that row, too!

After band practice, I went with all the fifth graders to see which teacher I would have for the coming school year. We all stood crowded in one of the fifth-grade classrooms that was in the basement of the school. It was a big classroom but seemed small when packed with so many people. I hoped that this room wouldn't be my classroom because it was impossible to see outside. Again, the classroom was in the basement of the school. As a teacher called a long list of names, students lined up and left to go to another classroom. Then another long list of names was called and those students left to go to another classroom. Thirty of us remained, and this was our classroom. I ended up getting Miss McCauley, the same teacher my sister had in fifth grade two years ago. I heard that Miss McCauley was a very strict teacher and gave lots of homework every night. The strictness didn't bother me at all. In fact, I welcomed it since I knew how to behave well. I hated homework, though.

When Miss McCauley started talking to us, her big body stood still in front of us. The only parts of her body that moved were her mouth and all the flab beneath her chin. During this first talk to the class, she explained that she had an "A" row, a "B" row, a "C" row, and a "D" row. Like me, I'm sure the other students were wondering where the "F" row was. She never mentioned it, though. In a way, it was comforting that she didn't have an "F" row. Possibly, because of the row Sue might have been in, Sue never told me about these rows. I don't know. Anyway, the teacher placed us in a seating order, which she said was determined by our last year's report card average. The teacher explained that if we didn't like the row or seat we were in, the only way to move up would be to work hard every day.

When Miss McCauley assigned seats, I was shocked to find myself given the third seat in the "A" row. Of course, this only meant that I had the third best report card average out of these thirty kids in fourth grade last year, not out of last year's entire fourth grade. Almost as interested in where I ended up sitting, I was curious to see where my two close friends in the class would sit. Chuck ended up sitting in the fourth seat in the "B" row, and Ray was given the next to the last desk in the "D" row. I really felt bad for Ray. He really seemed to be much brighter than that. Nevertheless, that was his assigned seat until the first report card of the year would come out.

According to Miss McCauley, that is when she would figure new averages on each of us and reassign seats.

After Miss McCauley assigned seats, she asked a few of us in the first row to help her hand out books. She asked me to hand out the math books. When I walked over to get the books, she asked me, "You're Susan's brother, aren't you?" I said, "Yes." That was all she said. As I put a math book on each student's desk, I made sure I gave myself one that looked like it was in decent shape. We were instructed to put our names on the inside cover of each book in ink on the next available line where names were already written from previous years. All of my books had at least four names inside of the cover already. My history book had more names than there were lines. The book had been around a long time. Yet, I liked receiving the books and checking the inside of the front covers to see who had used the books I was getting. As I wrote my name, Scott Paulson, in each book, I filled in the school year, too. I wrote 1960-1961, as I would be in possession of the books from September of 1960 until May of 1961. At our school, the school year always started the day after Labor Day in early September, and it usually ended sometime right before or right after Memorial Day in May. Next, there was a space to write the condition of the book. For the condition of each textbook, there was an option of writing one of the following descriptions of the book: new, good, fair, or poor. I don't remember ever putting the word new or good in that space in any book I ever got. Again, this year, I only wrote fair or poor because other students had always used my books. On rare occasion, as I did with the history book I got this year, I wrote that the book was in very poor condition. I don't remember ever getting a brand new schoolbook in grade school. Writing the condition of the book was a matter of opinion, anyway. Even if a book looked somewhat good, it probably wouldn't look good by the end of the school year after I would have carried it home and back many times through the school year. I wouldn't want anyone to blame me for making my books look worse than good just because I'd have to put some miles on them. Another reason my books may have not looked good by the end of the school year was that I hated using book covers. Like artwork, book covers were too much of a hassle. I tried using them in earlier grades, but they wouldn't stay on well. Finally, when I'd get my books each school year, I read the names of the students who had my books in previous years to see if I knew anyone who had used the book. I always thought I might get one of the books my sister used when she was in my grade. However, that never happened.

After Miss McCauley lined us up and took us to the bathroom and to a water faucet down the hall, she brought us back into the classroom and wrote a list on the blackboard with white chalk. It was a school supply list. The list was predictable. Everything she wrote on the board was something that my parents had already got for me to use in school. In fact, my parents bought me a few things that weren't on the list, like my own small pencil sharpener to keep in my desk. Miss McCauley told us to write the list on a sheet of paper and to take it home to our parents. If our parents couldn't send us to school with the supplies by the next day, Miss McCauley told us to come back tomorrow with the list signed by our parents. Obviously, she wanted to make sure that our parents had seen the list, even if everyone's parents couldn't get the supplies by the next day.

As I had expected, she told us to take out a sheet of paper or borrow a sheet of paper from someone if we didn't bring any paper to school yet. She said the same for a pencil. Chuck reached across the aisle, tapped me on the right arm, and said, "Psst! Lend me paper and a pencil." I gave him two sheets of paper and a pencil while knowing that he would probably never return it. That was all right, though. I didn't mind. I also gave him my pencil sharpener since the pencil hadn't been sharpened yet. I figured she was going to tell us to write about our summer. I was right.

After quickly writing the essay, I looked at the last few pages of the math book. I looked at the review pages at the end of the book, and I solved some of the math problems. There was another page to turn to for checking to see if the answers were correct. I did well. I figured that math class would be a breeze for me again. After looking at the math book, I opened the reading book to the last story. I thought that the length of the last story could give me some idea as to how difficult the reading book was going to be. I wasn't sure if the last story's length was a good indicator of the book's difficulty, but I thought it logically might be. After all, in previous grades, the last story in the book was the longest story in the book, and I didn't think the fifth grade reader would be any different. Also, by skimming the last story in the reader, I had some idea as to how well I would be able to read by the end of the school year.

I discreetly looked around and, as far as I could tell, I was the only student who even opened any books, let alone analyzed the ends of two of the books. Being so analytical made me feel like I was an unusual kid, maybe even weird. However, I never opened the remaining books, history and science, on that first day. I would let them sit inside my desk and gather dust until the teacher instructed us to open them. Even when I would have to open them, my mind would probably be somewhere else. I didn't care for reading history books, and I liked reading about science even less.

While some kids looked like they were about to fall asleep, I kept myself awake by wondering when it was time for recess in this classroom. Then I broke into a cold sweat as I thought that fifth graders might not get a recess as I had in previous years. That fear turned into somewhat of a reality. Though we had a 15-minute recess every school day during the first week of school, the class learned during the second week that recess wasn't guaranteed in Miss McCauley's class. When she was mad at us, we had no recess. Instead, she would line us up to go to the washroom and maybe to the drinking fountain. That was it. Then, when we got back in the classroom, she would sternly say, "I want all of you to spend your recess time thinking about the wrong you've done." Then we would sit silently for a while and think about the wrong we had done. The problem was that I didn't know what we had done wrong most of the times we were denied recess. She never told us. Wisely, no one ever asked her what we had done wrong. That probably would have cancelled recess for the next school day, too. The days without recess were a bummer because the 15-minute recess was something I liked about school, as it was time when I could get out of the room, not think about schoolwork or the wrong the class had apparently done, and get some fresh air.

After that first day of school, my sister was going to a friend's house before going home. So, I walked home alone. After-school activities hadn't started yet, so I could go home right at three o'clock. When I got home, I walked in the kitchen where Mom was preparing dinner. I told her that Miss McCauley was my teacher. She dropped her cooking utensils on the counter and screeched, "Oh, no! Don't tell me!" With a red face, she said loudly with a determined voice, "I'm calling that school tomorrow and having you moved to another class immediately, Scott!" No doubt, Mom was very unhappy with Miss McCauley's performance when Sue had her for a teacher two years ago.

As always, at five o'clock, we were waiting at the dinner table for Dad to come home from the office. He walked in and kissed Mom on the cheek while making a loud and comical smooching sound to humor us. Then he hugged her. Sensing she had something on her mind, he softly asked, "Something wrong, hon?" She said, "I'll tell you later." Then Dad smiled at each of us three kids, got his usual huge hug from Sue, and started asking us about our first day at school while Mom took dinner off the stove and out of the oven. This particular night, Mom made my favorite dinner, which was her homemade spaghetti and hot biscuits. To make the meal even better, there were no vegetables in sight. I always wanted the parts of the spaghetti from the skillet that had the largest amounts of gooey cheese melted on it. I reminded Mom of this as she started dishing out the spaghetti. After sprinkling lots of Parmesan cheese on the spaghetti, I dug into the steaming plate of delicious food. Mom said, "I always love to cook for Scott. Nobody enjoys food more than he does." Sue and Brett snickered. Dad quickly silenced my bone-thin brother, who I envied for never gaining a pound regardless of what he stuffed in his face, as well as my sister. Dad never allowed us to make fun of one another.

After I told my dad that my teacher was Miss McCauley, my teacher became the topic of discussion during the rest of the dinner. Mom insisted that she was going to either go to the school or call the school tomorrow to get me out of that class. Sensing that I wanted to stay in Miss McCauley's class, Dad suggested that Mom leave it alone for a while. He told Mom, "Old McCauley may do better with Scott than she did with Sue, hon." I tried backing Dad's support and added, "You know, Miss McCauley remembers Sue." With disgust, Mom said, "I bet she does. I bet she'll never forget me either." I said, "I think she liked Sue." With an angry look, Mom just shook her head slowly from left to right as she stared into Dad's eyes. She had the look she sometimes had when I wouldn't want to hear what she was going to say next. Then she snapped, "That woman just sat at her desk, day after day, and made the kids do busy work. She never taught Sue a thing." Dad told Mom, "I think you're being too hard on the woman, hon," and then asked Sue what she thought of Miss McCauley. She said, "She was okay, but she never let us talk. If we did, she yelled at us." Knowing how much Sue and her girlfriends talked, they probably were yelled at a lot.

After hearing all of this, I really wanted to stay in Miss McCauley's room. After all, sitting in a room and doing work all day, with kids who were afraid of misbehaving, sounded very comforting to me. Even the name-calling bullies that I didn't like wouldn't be able to talk in this classroom. Nobody would dare try to call me names or throw fat jokes my way. As fat as Miss McCauley was, fat talk would be forbidden. Besides being huge, she was probably almost as old as my grandma and had a very mean look on her face, much like a bulldog that was expected to bark at any second. She was perfect for intimidating bad kids, which would make good kids feel safe from bad kids. Additionally, since Chuck and Ray were in my class, I thought I would have plenty of support if bad times were to come my way. I most certainly would have sided with them if anyone were to pick on them. Last but not least, I was the third smartest student in there. Though I knew I wasn't a genius, I felt great about being in the "A" row and about the class's apparent lack of academic competition.

Before going to bed that night, I put my hand up to Brett's face to make sure he was asleep in his bottom bunk of our bunk beds. If he didn't yell or hit me, he was asleep. Since he didn't move, I was positive that he wouldn't see or hear me. My test to see if he was sleeping was foolproof. Next, I planted both of my knees firmly on the floor. Then I clasped my hands tightly together, looked up to the dark ceiling, and softly said, "You've got to really pay attention to me tonight, Jesus." Next, I lowered my head, closed my eyes as tight as I could and said my prayers. At the end of my prayers, I begged to stay in Miss McCauley's classroom. Besides being a comfortable class for me, I would be with Chuck and Ray. I could also quietly do my work every day and then, when finished, let my daydreams run wild. I didn't know if that's what the Lord would want to hear, but it was true. I loved to daydream at school, and I found that rowdy classes made it impossible to do. This class wouldn't be very rowdy at all. Even though it may have been selfish to pray for something that Mom didn't want, I prayed for what I wanted in hopes of having the best school year possible.

After pleading with the Lord, I quietly climbed up to the top bunk and thought about my daydreaming habit. I hadn't done any serious daydreaming since I left Mrs. Lindsay's fourth grade class last May, and I knew there must be many places my daydreams hadn't taken me yet. Now, if Mom would just let me stay in Miss McCauley's classroom, I would have a chance to go to more of those places.

Chapter Three: Riverview Amusement Park

The first week of school quickly passed. Since I was still in Miss McCauley's class, I could only assume that Mom listened to Dad's advice and had not called Mr. Monge, the school's principal, to have my class changed. I hoped more than ever that she wouldn't because Miss McCauley seemed very nice, so far, and seemed to like me. As I had predicted, I was very comfortable in her classroom. Again, another advantage to being in this classroom was that I got to sit close to my best friend, Chuck. In addition, being in the "A" row was as big a thrill to me as I had originally thought it would be. I really liked this "A" row, "B" row "C" row, and "D" row arrangement. If Miss McCauley's goal was to get kids to work hard by seating us this way, she had succeeded with me. I was trying to do my very best.

I enjoyed the first week of band practice a lot. As I recall, the band went outside and marched around the streets of the school every morning except the first day of school during the first week. We were practicing for the best band event of the year. This event made the early morning wake up calls from Mom and the eight o'clock band rehearsals worthwhile. Every year, during a weekend in September, our band participated in the Mardi Gras Parade competition at Riverview Amusement Park. Riverview was world renowned for its many different rides, games, and other forms of entertainment. I had heard that many famous people had been there. It was located at the intersection of Belmont and Ashland Avenues in Chicago, probably a little more than an hour's drive to the northeast from my school in Joliet.

When we went on this particular year, the band met at the school by 4:30 in the afternoon. As always, Mr. Mattei instructed the bus driver to leave within ten minutes of his announced departure time. Mr. Mattei always thought people should be prompt or miss life's offerings. No one was ever late when we headed to Riverview. In fact, most of us were at the school waiting to board the bus by 4:15. Everyone wanted to go on this band trip.

The only bad part of the whole evening was the discomfort in wearing the band uniform. It was made of wool, which meant it was hot and heavy. The uniform looked nice, though. The dark blue jacket and pants made it appear distinguished. The jacket's big gold-colored buttons down the front and bright gold-colored braids hanging on the shoulders gave the outfit a royal look. The pants had gold-colored stripes along the outer seams. The matching hat had a huge golden plume sticking up in the front of it. We had to wear our own white shirt, black tie, and black shoes and socks with the uniform. Dad tried to teach me how to tie a tie, but I couldn't do it well. So, he tied my tie around my neck at home. He let it hang loosely so I would be comfortable until I would have to tighten it just before the performance. After the performance, naturally, I'd loosen it and take it off. Also on our jackets, we would wear the medals we had earned in band contests. So far, I had received eight first place medals, one-second place, and no third place. The second place was my debut solo contest in second grade. In every other contest performance, whether it was with or without the band, in an ensemble or playing a solo, I had gotten a first place. By six o'clock, we were in marching band formation, ready and eager to perform for the massive crowds at the park that evening. Within forty-five minutes, we had marched around the park, played several marches repeatedly, and returned to the bus. The girls got on the bus to change to their street clothes. After the last girl had finished, the boys took their turn to change clothes on the bus, which only was lit by the exit sign in the back of the bus. I dillydallied around so I could change last. I didn't want anyone to see that I wore long johns under my uniform since the uniform's woolen pants made me itch so much. Being early September, it was obviously weird to be wearing long johns because it was too warm out to do so. After I changed and got off the bus, I found my sister and her friend Donna anxiously waiting for me. We found Mr. Mattei stationed a short distance from the bus as he was handing out a roll of tickets to each band member. There was one ticket for almost every ride in the park.

I didn't mind that Sue had a friend with her, especially since it could mean more tickets for me. Girls usually didn't like the fast roller coasters, and they would either throw those tickets away, trade them for some of the milder rides, or give them to boys. Sure enough, Sue and Donna both gave me their tickets to the Bobs, the fastest roller coaster in the park. In turn, I gave them my tickets to things that were less exciting to me. Since they were nice enough to exchange some tickets with me, I thought it was only proper to stay with them for a while. It's a place where girls didn't mind being seen with any boy, even if the boy was a girl's little brother. Girls were most likely too afraid of strangers to be on their own. We boys probably should have been frightened, too, but it didn't seem as though we were. Though I was a very shy kid, I was hardly ever afraid. After all, I had a watch on my wrist and knew what time I had to be back on the bus. Girls are most likely more cautious or maybe they're just smarter than boys are at young ages. I don't know.

First, Sue asked me to take her and her friend to the ride I discovered last year. I said, "Oh, you mean the one where the floor drops out from under you?" "Yeah," she said, "that's the one! What's it called?" I said, "I'm not sure, but I think it's called The Rotor or something like that. It was really good." I had talked about it several times since I was on it last year after the band had come to Riverview. The ride wasn't far from the bus, and the line of people waiting to get on it wasn't too long. So, we watched one group of people take their places with their backs against the wall of the huge cylinder. The cylinder slowly started to turn and the people began to scream in anticipation of what was about to happen. The ride started spinning the people around faster and faster. Then the floor started to drop out from under them. Their backs were pinned up against the wall inside the cylinder. Heavy people sank a little bit, but most people didn't slide down the wall at all. They just stayed pressed against the wall. Then after several minutes, the floor came back up and the cylinder started slowing down gradually. Finally, the ride came to a complete stop.

On a microphone, the ride operator said, "Everyone please exit at the gate. And please, ladies and gentlemen, boys and girls, watch your step as you leave." The people stumbled and staggered across the floor of the big cylinder toward the gate. It was funny seeing the people, still dizzy from the spinning cylinder ride, walk as if they were drunk.

Then Donna and I handed the man at the gate our tickets and got in the cylinder with about fifteen other people. Sue chickened out, saying, "I'll meet you two over there at the exit." And, she was gone! During the ride, Donna and I laughed and laughed while the others either laughed or screamed until the ride ended. Then like the people before us, we staggered from the dizziness of the ride to the exit gate like stumbling drunks. Even though this girlfriend of Sue's wasn't my friend, it seemed like I was having more fun with her than Sue was. I knew that would have to change.

To make sure Sue had some fun with Donna, I said I wanted to go on the Bobs next. I knew this would be my chance to get away and to make sure they started having some fun together. But Donna and Sue talked me out of going on the Bobs just yet. They still weren't ready to go it alone in this big park, I guess. Therefore, I scrutinized my roll of tickets and said, "We have a new ticket this year. It sounds like a tame ride. Even though it's called the Wild Mouse, I bet it has something to do with Mickey Mouse. It's got to be an easy ride, don't you think?" The girls weren't so sure but were willing to try it.

After we found the ride, it didn't look quite as tame as I had imagined it to be. But I was never intimidated by the roller coasters and thought this would be nothing compared to the Bobs. I figured this would be a medium speed ride, a good one for breaking Sue into the more advanced world of roller coasters. After much convincing talk from Donna and me, Sue got in one mouse car with me. Maybe she felt safer with me on this ride than with Donna. I don't know. Donna got in the one behind us. Since there was a long line, the man who was collecting the tickets at the gate told people that there had to be two people in each mouse car. Therefore, Donna had to sit with a stranger. The stranger was a guy who looked just a little older than she was. Therefore, she didn't seem to mind. As some people tried to be in a mouse car by themselves, the man operating the ride firmly announced, "No solos! If you want to have a seat to yourself, you'll have to come back when we're not so busy." I was glad I got to sit with Sue because I wouldn't have wanted to sit with someone I didn't know. If I had to, though, I would have.

The ride took off very slowly and went down a long track as Sue sat rigidly in front of me leaning back into my chest. At the end of the track, without warning, there was a sharp turn. My heart skipped a beat as Sue fell limp in my arms. She had fainted! Not sure of what this ride was going to do next, I just held Sue and patted her cheek while saying, "Wake up, Sue! C'mon, now, wake up!" Screaming for help wouldn't have done any good, obviously, since the guy in control of the ride was back at the starting point. No one could help me out on the track of the roller coaster ride. As Sue limply continued leaning back against me, the mouse car went even faster and took a few more unsuspected turns, which made my heart skip a few more beats. Though I don't remember the ride going real high like the Bobs, it wasn't without its surprises as it had one surprising sharp turn after another. Finally, I saw the ramp ahead where people were watching and waiting for their turn to get on the Wild Mouse. The mouse car slowed down and came to a halt. Just when I figured there would be no more surprises, I got a delightful surprise. Sue spoke. She asked, "Are we done already?" I just told her to get off the ride. She persisted, "Tell me. What happened? Is the ride over already?" I said, "I'll tell you later. Just go!" Donna came up to us from behind and asked, "Sue, are you all right? You're all white." Then Donna turned to me and said, "She must have been frightened." When we got back to ground level a short distance from the ride, I told them what had happened.

At this, Donna started acting motherly towards Sue. Since I knew Sue was all right and the two girls now had plenty to talk about, I finally had a chance to head for the big one. I told them I would meet them back behind the Wild Mouse in about a half-an-hour or so and then dashed off to the Bobs to use all three tickets! Besides mine, I had their tickets for the Bobs, too. "Sure, sure, whenever," said Donna as she continued to rehash the last five minutes of poor Sue's life on the Wild Mouse.

I truly enjoyed conquering the challenge of going on the Bobs every year. I felt my racing heart beat faster and faster as the linked cars chugged up the steep hills made of wood. My insides felt as though they were turned upside down as the roller coaster reached the highest peak, which was 87 feet high in the air, and started down the steep track. When the ride cruised down 85 feet from its high point, it would reach a speed of 50 miles an hour. Though it might not sound very fast, it actually was very fast for the short distance back down near the ground. Then as the ride headed to the tunnel, there were huge warning signs that read, "Stay in Your Seat! Do Not Stand Up!" There were rumors of people standing up during the Bobs' journey and being decapitated by the overhead entrance to the tunnel. I hoped that was just a juicy rumor and wasn't true. If it were true, I definitely wouldn't want the people in front of me to stand up because that would have been way too gross for me. The few seconds spent entering and going through the tunnel were the most dangerous, yet the most exciting part of the roller coaster ride. The risk of going on the Bobs was always my biggest thrill. After three times on the Bobs, I could rate this year's trip as excellent.

On the way back to the Wild Mouse, I stopped at the Freak House. It was hard to miss since the man on the stage in front of the Freak House was yelling into a megaphone, "Step right up, folks, and see some of the world's most unbelievable sights. You'll never see anything like this again in your entire life." As he pointed to the curtained stage, he continued by saying, "In here, you'll see some of the most hideous-looking creatures on earth! Just to whet your appetites, I'm going to bring out one of the performers now." A midget walked out on stage as the crowd gasped and sighed with sympathy. He was not only a midget, but he also was deformed with bow-legged legs and crippled hands. Then again, I didn't know if that's just how he was acting or if that's how he really was. In case the audience didn't notice the deformities themselves, the emcee pointed to each deformity with a varnished wooden pointer as he shouted the details out to the crowd through the megaphone. Even though the performer was extremely short, he was a good-looking man. The emcee was ugly, though. Anyway, I couldn't imagine paying money to see more people like this inside the Freak House, even if I'd had enough money. However, there were obviously people who didn't feel as I did as many people lined up to get in.

The only positive thing about all of this was that these unfortunate human beings would be paid for doing nothing more than standing there and being observed by the curious people. At least they had easy jobs. Feeling bad for the performers in this attraction, I backed away while still looking at the midget on stage, and then turned to start walking back to the Wild Mouse where I had promised to meet Sue and Donna. On the way, I stopped to watch some lady stand under a healthy stream of air, which made her skirt fly up to expose her underwear. I remembered seeing some silly thing like that on television or in a movie before. Actually, it didn't appear as though the lady who was doing it here was much of a lady at all. People stood around and laughed at her. A few older guys whistled real loud at her. I didn't know what the big deal was. If people wanted to see a girl in underwear, all they'd have to do is come to our house on a morning when my sister was running later than usual. She'd be running up and down the hallway from the bathroom to her bedroom in a panic as she tried to do her hair and get her clothes color-coordinated at the same time.

Anyway, I found Sue and Donna near the Wild Mouse. They were watching a guy, who I think was called Bozo, by the guy who was running the game. Or, maybe the girls were watching the boys who were playing the game that featured Bozo. Bozo sat on a board above a big tank of water. He would insult the people who were paying money to throw balls at a huge disk next to the water tank. If someone were to hit the big disk hard enough with the ball, the board that Bozo was sitting on would collapse and he would fall into the big tank of water. Bozo insulted the guys by saying things like, "You can't throw!" Or he would shout, "Hey, big fella, you throw like my little sister!" Of course, the more he insulted the guys, the more the guys with money would pay to try dunking him in the water. Whether they were able to dunk him or not, Bozo and the announcer ended up with their money. After we finally saw someone throw good and hard enough to knock Bozo off his seat and into the water, we started leaving. As we walked away, we heard Bozo yelling some more, "You were lucky! You threw that pitch like my little sister! Bet you can't dunk me again! C'mon, prove you're a man!" I turned around to see if the guy was going to waste more money by trying to knock Bozo off the board again. He didn't. In hopes that others would part with their money, the drenched entertainer started insulting other guys who were standing around his game area instead.

Not far from there, we saw a man trying to guess people's weight. Of course, he took some money from people before he guessed their weight. If the man was more than a few pounds off, the people got a stuffed animal. If the man guessed within a few pounds of their weight, the people just lost their money. While we watched, the man guessed two people's weights within a few pounds. I don't know how he did it. He would put his fingertips to his chin, look the people up and down, and say, "Let me see now." Then he would guess a number. The people would get on the scale and lose their money. I wondered if the scale was set to stop at certain numbers. Being suspicious of how he could guess different people's weights so accurately, I thought the game was rigged somehow. It was games like this that made me think people would spend money on practically anything at this park. Anyway, even if I had had the money to play this game, I wouldn't have because the crowd watching would then know my weight. To me, that was personal.

The object of the next game we saw was to ring a bell at the top of a long pole with the metal disk, which jumped when the player's mallet struck the pad. If a person were to ring the bell, he would get a big stuffed animal for his girlfriend or for himself. Unlike the Bozo game, the man who encouraged the people to play this game didn't insult the players. He said, "Step right up and show everyone just how strong you are. Flex your muscular arms and swing the mallet." Then he would swing the mallet himself to show everyone that it could be done. Though this game looked more legitimate than some other games looked, I thought this game might be rigged so that it worked somehow for the carnival worker but not for the people paying to play for prizes. While we were there, the worker pointed at a guy with a girl in the crowd and ask, "How about you? I bet your pretty little lady there would love to see you win one of these mementos of your strength for her." As he said this, he held up a huge stuffed animal. It was a big purple thing, which I didn't think resembled any animal I had ever seen. Then, the huge guy in the crowd agreed to try ringing the bell to win the stuffed animal. Of course, he had to pay a dollar for the three chances to ring the bell way up in the air on top of the long pole. He hit the pad hard three times, and the disk went very high all three times. However, he lost as the disk never made it to the very top to ring the bell. Very few people ever rang the bell when I had watched them play this game. It was apparently a tough game to win. Or, as I said, it may have been fixed somehow to only ring when the worker swung the mallet. Though I was curious to see how high I could make the metal disk rise up towards the bell, I wasn't curious enough to spend a dollar and possibly embarrass myself in front of everyone who would be watching me.

Finally, I found the game I enjoyed watching the most last year when the band came to the park. I think Mouse Run was the name of this one. Sue and Donna said they would walk slowly ahead because they didn't want to look at a mouse. I didn't really care to look at a mouse either, but I sure liked watching this game. The game had a large round platform with lots of small holes around the edge of it. In the middle of the platform, all I could see was a metal bowl turned upside down with a couple small holes in it. Everyone knew that there was a live mouse under the bowl, waiting to be released. The people playing the game would bet on which of the many holes the mouse would run to after the man removed the bowl. This year, like last year, it was obvious that the mouse was not running to the holes that many people had bet on. Therefore, the man in charge of the game would never have to give out many prizes. Like Bozo and the man with the mallet, he would just keep the profits.

I decided to watch the actions of the man running the game very closely rather than watch the mouse. Maybe, I thought, I could see if this game was designed to cheat people, just as I had suspected the weight-guessing game was designed to cheat the people who played for cash. As I watched, I noticed that every time the man reached over the platform to uncover the mouse, he pressed two fingers of his left hand very hard on the edge of one of the holes that hardly anyone had bet on. Then, he would stall by asking repeatedly, "No more bets? Are you sure, ladies and gentlemen? No more bets?" Then he'd instruct them, "Everyone must stand up straight and not lean against the platform." He said that distracting the mouse could disqualify a person from winning.

Every time, the mouse ran to the hole that the man had touched. I worked my way through the small crowd and got right next to the man running the game. When I put my face down by the last hole he had rubbed, the man pushed me hard with his elbow to get me away from the hole. When I defiantly pushed back to where I was, he pushed me even harder with his hand. That was his mistake because I could then smell vinegar on his hand. The vinegar was apparently making the mouse run where the man wanted it to run. I quickly worked my way to the back of the circular crowd and waited for them to get quiet just before the next mouse would run. After looking around to make sure I didn't know anyone near me, I disguised my voice by making a growling sound in my throat. Then I yelled in a hoarse voice, "He's a cheat! He puts vinegar on the hole. He's a cheat!" As the crowd began talking loudly in response to what I yelled, I ran like I hadn't run in a while. I don't know if the people who placed bets ever proved my claim, but I hope they did. I never liked liars and cheaters. I rarely had ever done anything this gutsy before. Therefore, besides feeling a little afraid, I was feeling quite proud of myself.

In fact, after three trips on the Bobs and then thinking I was the Mouse Run fools' savior, I was feeling like the king of the park. However, I stifled this feeling when I caught up with Sue and Donna because I knew I wouldn't do anything gutsy around them. After all, taking chances in front of people I knew wasn't allowed with my shyness. I hate to say that I almost always had to be alone to have lots of fun, but sometimes, that's how it was. I really hated being shy around people I knew, but I just felt I couldn't help it. The girls and I looked at our remaining tickets and headed toward the Pair-o-Chutes, which were a pair of parachutes standing side by side at the far end of the park. They looked so harmless and boring. As Sue and I got in the bucket of one of the parachutes, the man operating the ride strapped us in place securely. First, he told us to sit still. Next, he said, "There's a pause when you reach the top, then there's a jolt just before the bucket starts falling with the parachute opening over your heads. Hold on!"

My eyes must have looked terrified at this last command because the guy looked me in the eyes and said, "Not to worry, kid. You'll enjoy it. You can see the whole park from up there." I assured him that I could handle anything. "After all," I told the man, "I was just on the Bobs three times in the last couple of hours." He slapped my knee and said, "Well, this should be a breeze for you then." From his laugh, he seemed to enjoy his unintentional pun. Up we went. Though I felt like he was patronizing me like an adult would when trying to sooth a child's fears, I couldn't help but feel awkward on this ride. As I looked down at Donna, who was waiting on the ground with another stranger for the next parachute ride, I saw her getting smaller and smaller and smaller as Sue and I were going higher and higher and higher. The smaller Donna got, the more I felt sick to my stomach. I was really getting uncomfortable as we moved upward very slowly while being suspended in the air in this bucket seat. Sue looked at me and asked, "Are you all right, Scott?" I said, "Not really." She firmly threatened, "You better not faint up here. You'll fall!" That was the worst thing she could have said. I was then not only afraid of being suspended in air but also frightened of being frightened.

What a time and place to discover that I was afraid of heights. I didn't know why, but I was really enjoying high rides like the Bobs, which were moving fast, and letting the wild wind blow against my face. However, this slow climb to the top of the parachute ride was killing me inside. I felt like I wanted to jump just to get off the thing, but I knew I couldn't do that. When we finally got near the top, I remembered what the man below had said. So I opened my eyes and tried to enjoy the scenery of the entire park. I hoped that would replace my fears. However, looking out over the huge amusement park was a mistake. It was one of the most frightening things I had ever seen. The park was really, really far below me. Looking down at it made my stomach twist and turn more than it did on the Bobs or the Wild Mouse.

I closed my eyes again very tightly. Then I felt the bucket jolt, as the man said it would, and I muttered, "Lord, be with me!" Then, the cool part of the ride finally occurred as the bucket and opened parachute over our heads glided to the ground. I enjoyed the fall almost as much as riding on the Bobs. Descending in the parachute made my insides feel like they felt when Dad drove over the bridges in Joliet too fast. It was great. Just as we would reach the top of the arched bridge and drive down the far side of the bridge, my whole body felt weird. As much as I loved the parachute's fall, though, I knew I would never go on one of these rides again. My fear during the parachute's slow climb made me vow never to put myself through it again. Getting out of the parachute ride, Sue said, "That ride's okay." I said nothing about it. It seemed strange that I loved being high in the air on the rollercoasters that kept moving fast, but I couldn't stand to be sitting motionless up high in an open bucket on the parachute ride.

As we walked past the Ferris wheel, we checked our tickets and saw we had tickets for this tame-looking ride. Though I had been on much smaller Ferris wheels many times before, this big one ended up bothering me after having just been on the Pair-o-Chutes. As all three of us got in the bucket seat, the man closed the metal bar in front of our waists. The wheel began to turn, and then stopped about a tenth of the way around so that the next group of people in line could get in another bucket. By the time we reached the top and the Ferris wheel stopped to let more people in other buckets, I started having haunting, terrifying memories of waiting for the parachute to fall. Naturally, it was a memory I wanted to forget. However, I couldn't forget it, and it ruined this ride for me. On the rollercoasters, as long as the ride was moving, I wasn't feeling bad regardless of the height. However, when I was sitting still way up high, I wasn't comfortable at all.

Unfortunately, after going around and around on the Ferris wheel many times, the bucket that we were in was positioned to let us off last. That meant that the wheel would turn just a little to let one bucket clear out and then let more people get on. If I had counted right, Sue, Donna and I would have to stop ten times before we'd get off the thing. Of course, some of the stops would be very high in the air. Naturally, one of the stops to let some people off and others on had us suspended in the air at the highest point of the Ferris wheel again. Being on an end of our bucket and not wanting to let the girls know I was afraid, I just positioned my head as though I was looking down to the side of the bucket. But my eyes were closed very tight like they were on the parachute ride before it eased back to the ground. I assumed that they couldn't see that I closed my eyes from where they were. After all, I was embarrassed about my newly found fear of heights that only tormented me when I was suspended motionless in air. When we finally got off the ride, I extended my secret promise to myself. Not only would I never go on the parachute again, but I would never go on the huge Ferris wheel again either. Any ride that stopped high in the air and had me practically dangling in midair was out from now on. Sue could have all those tickets if she wanted them.

Next, we went on one of my favorite rides, the Tilt-a-Whirl. On the Tilt-a-Whirl, up to five people or so would sit in one of several huge things that looked like a bucket. The buckets would travel around in a huge circle. While the bucket slowly went around in a circle, it would slightly incline and decline, which made the bucket twirl around. If people leaned one way or another in the bucket, sometimes it would help the bucket spin more. Though it was a gentle ride, I liked it a great deal.

Then I went off on my own for a short time again. I debated going in the fun house called Aladdin's Castle like I did last year, but decided to use my time hitting a few more roller coasters. Lines were too long at the Jetstream, so I went on the Flying Turns and the Comet instead. I had forgotten how much I enjoyed the Comet until I had experienced it again, and I put it on my list of favorites with the Bobs and now the Wild Mouse. There were a few roller coasters that we didn't have tickets for, so I'd have to try them another year. The ones I knew by name were called the Big Dipper, Skyrocket, Pippin, and Gee Wiz. In time, I figured I would be able to try them all since the school band came here every September.

Glad that Sue and Donna really enjoyed my company as we went around the park, I didn't mind spending the remaining time with them at all. We walked around looking at the different things that took money instead of tickets. Without money, of course, we were observers rather than participants. In the carnival area of the park, there were a lot more games like the Mouse Run and the Bozo game to watch. Sue and I ignored the many concession stands selling food since we didn't have more than a couple bucks between us. Donna, however, did have quite a bit of money, and she bought pink cotton candy. They gave her a big ball of the sticky, sugary stuff on a long white paper cone. She offered us some. I tore off a little bit and balled it up before I put it in my mouth. The sugar crystals felt gritty, and I didn't want the gritty, lose candy on my tongue. It felt weird to me. I preferred that it would be packed tightly together. Due to its awkward texture, I never liked cotton candy very much and therefore didn't have any more when Donna offered it. Both Sue and Donna really seemed to like the taste of it, though. They ate it all. Even though it's one of my least favorite sugary things to eat, it's fun to watch people eat it. Sue and Donna looked like they were inhaling clouds.

As we continued walking toward the bus, we watched people exiting the Haunted House. They always acted as if it was so scary. I knew it probably wasn't scary at all because I'd been to Haunted Houses at other places, and they were funny rather than scary. There were no ghosts in those places. It was regular people in there trying to make people think it was a scary place. In my opinion, it was a waste of time and money. To me, the great places to be that weren't a waste of time and money at Riverview were on the roller coasters. But, I had used up almost all the tickets. The only ones left were for the two rides in which the lines of people waiting to get on the rides were too long. We had a time limit to get back to the bus.

During the bus ride home, it was quiet. Being late for school kids to be up, almost eleven o'clock, many slept on the way home. I could never sleep well away from home, though, so I stayed awake. I always sat near the front of the bus on these trips because, according to Mom, it was supposed to ease my carsickness. Sometimes my mom referred to it as motion sickness. When I took long trips, I would get real bad headaches and feel nauseated. Mom read somewhere that the motion of the vehicle caused the headaches. Since most of the motion of a vehicle is in the back, especially when it hits bumps or makes wide turns, I sat in the front of the bus as often as I could. Most kids liked sitting away from the bus driver and the adult supervisors who would sit near the front, anyway. Therefore, it wasn't difficult to find a seat near the front. Mr. Mattei talked to a couple of us kids as we inched through Chicago traffic to head home. He said that Riverview had opened in 1904 and that he came to Riverview with his buddies when he was younger. When he said that the park opened in 1904, I thought about Grandpa who would have been older than Riverview if he were still alive. Mr. Mattei said the park seemed further away from Joliet back then than it does these days. He said that we were spoiled by coming on a school bus. Back in the day, he had to come by train from Joliet to Chicago with his friends, and then they had to continue their journey to the park. He also told us that bringing the band to Riverview was always his favorite band activity of the year because he loved seeing us kids have such a good time.

As the bus drove us home, I thought about the new roller coaster ride I rode on, the Wild Mouse. In spite of Sue fainting, I was thinking about how exciting it was. This ride was a real thrill for me since I never knew what to expect next, thanks to its sudden twists and sharp turns. I wanted every second of the day, every day, to be as unpredictably fascinating as riding on the Wild Mouse. Of course, life has its slow days, too. Few days were as exciting as a roller coaster ride, but I'd just have to hold on until I'd find my next opportunity for such excitement. When we arrived back at school, many cars were waiting for the bus to return. Sue and I got in Dad's car. Dad looked so tired. Yet, he never, ever complained about doing things for us. Actually, I would have preferred the adventure of walking home that late, but he never would have allowed it.

Chapter Four: Activities

Weeks went by before Mom even asked how school was going for me. I no longer worried about having to change classes because Mom hadn't mentioned it since the first day of school. She apparently had other things on her mind. She had been different this school year by not asking about my homework almost daily. So far, she hadn't offered to help me with my homework or even ask me if I had any homework to do. Another thing that was different was that she didn't talk to me about joining activities. Instead, she just signed me up for things and told me when I should be there.

The biggest change in Mom was the way she didn't seem to worry about me as she did in the past. I assumed she still cared about me, but she wasn't worried. Though I liked how she wasn't worrying about me, it made me worry about her. I was concerned about why she wasn't acting like herself, and I was curious as to why she was acting differently, too.

For the first time ever, near the beginning of this school year, I heard Mom arguing with Dad. I didn't know why she would get so loud with him, but she did it a couple of times. I had only heard Mom get loud in anger with Brett and more often with me. Dad, however, never raised his voice back to her. If anything at all, he'd just be silent or respond in a soft and unhappy tone of voice. Mom seemed so unhappy and tired every evening. I assumed that Grandpa's death and caring for Grandma had much to do with it, if not everything to do with it. But I also couldn't help but wonder if Mom would ever be like she was before this past summer. I sure hoped she would be.

One morning on the way to band rehearsal, Sue mentioned Mom and Dad's arguments. She wiped tears from the corners of her eyes as she told me how she noticed Mom acting differently lately. Like kids do, I was quick to mention the frightful word, divorce. She didn't know if things were that bad. The more I thought about it, the more I hoped that we were just worrying too much about their arguments. This seemed serious, though, because Mom and Dad never argued in front of us before. From what I had heard from a couple of other kids at school, arguments between parents were a regular way of life at some houses. However, it was frighteningly foreign to the three of us kids in our house.

Every time I had heard the word divorce, I thought of Chuck. I didn't want my family to turn out like his. He lived with his sister, two brothers, and his mom in a small, rundown house at the edge of town. All he had ever said about his dad was that he thought he was living in California or some other faraway place. When I had visited Chuck in the past, his older sister, who was Sue's age, and his older brother, who was one year older than he was, were the ones in charge of the house. His mother and younger brother were rarely there. I figured that this was pretty much how it always was in divorced households. Of all the times I had been over to his house, I never smelled food cooking. I only saw him making his own baloney sandwiches and watched him argue with his sister when she wouldn't let him have snack foods. They never drank milk. The house was always dirty with crumb-filled plates and soda pop-stained drinking glasses sitting around in most every room. There were smelly clothes all over the floors of the living room, bathroom, and Chuck's bedroom. Everyone must have worn white socks because I saw them all over the place. They weren't real white like my sister's bobby socks. The socks at Chuck's were in need of soap, hot water, and bleach. When I had walked down the hallway to use their bathroom, I could see that beds never were made. I cringed when I saw bugs crawling up the walls or across the floor, and I saw many of them there. I sometimes wondered why Chuck would even ask me over when there was obviously so much work to do at his house. Rather than work inside the house or do other chores outside the house, he always preferred fooling around or wrestling with me.

His sister, Diane, would get the pillows out of the bedrooms and start playing with us if her older boyfriend wasn't around. She liked having playful pillow fights. When her boyfriend was there, she would yell at Chuck and me. She would yell, "Why don't you two grow up?" Then she would sit in the kitchen, staring at her boyfriend who appeared to be much too old for her. She took puffs on his cigarettes while he smoked and ate their snack foods. Even though she was in the same grade as my sister, I couldn't imagine Sue being anything like her. Sue talked about boys she thought were nice, but she never had them over to the house. I also knew that Sue would never smoke. It's too bad Diane acted that way because she was a pretty girl and, according to Chuck, she was smart. Anyway, Chuck's family was my only impression of a divorced home, and I didn't want to live like that.

Yet, Chuck was my best friend. I tried not thinking about how sorry I felt about his home life when we were together. I just enjoyed joking around with him. He didn't come to my house often. Maybe he sensed what I had thought since the first time I brought him home. Even though he was very polite to my mother, I don't think she liked him much. Also, I thought she was always watching him when he was over at our house, unlike she watched other kids who came over to see Sue, Brett, or me. Since he came from the neighborhood at the edge of town where houses weren't as nice as houses in our neighborhood, maybe she thought he was poor. Maybe she thought he would steal things from us. I'm not sure why she treated Chuck different than she treated all the other kids who came to our house, and, if I were to ask, I probably wouldn't have wanted to hear her answer. So, I never started that conversation with her. I knew that Chuck was okay, and I was positive that he would never do anything to embarrass me in front of my mom. Even though Mom didn't seem to like him, I wished he had come over to my house more, anyway, because it was a long walk for me to get to his house.

During the first several weeks of school, I saw that Mom was accurate in her assessment of Miss McCauley. Unless approached by students with questions, she just sat and read her newspapers at her desk in the front of the classroom. Sometimes I would see her writing, and after I went up to her desk with a question one day, I saw she was doing a crossword puzzle in the newspaper. She gave us a lot of work to do. The work that wasn't done in school was supposed to be completed for homework. With all the activities my parents had me signed up for, finding time to do the homework was difficult some evenings. To stay in the third seat in the "A" row, however, I was making myself find time to do the work. Being concerned about the way Mom was acting differently and me being so very busy with the schoolwork during the day, my hopes of pleasant daydreaming in the classroom weren't working out very well. I didn't totally sacrifice my enjoyment of daydreaming, however, as I sometimes did some daydreaming before I fell asleep in bed at night. That was night dreaming, I suppose, instead of daydreaming.

My schedule was probably as hectic as anyone's was. Besides having to get up by seven o'clock in the morning and get to band practice with Sue by eight o'clock every weekday, I had to attend school from nine o'clock until three in the afternoon. My parents often had me involved in the season's sports or activities after school. The sports' seasons usually didn't last all season for me, as I would be sent packing when the coaches would start cutting players to work exclusively with the good players they would use in the big competitions. Little did they realize that being kicked off the team was just fine with me. In most instances, it was just one less thing I had to think about and do. Yet, Mom told me that I needed to try every sport and activity to see if I would like one. She said that I might actually be good at a sport or activity after trying it and want to continue doing it.

In October, I started basketball for the first time. I didn't like to watch it, let alone play in a game. However, I did like some of the practice drills. Practice didn't let out until almost 4:30. Later in the season, when the days would shorten and it would get dark earlier, I'd get to walk home in the dark. Some street corners had streetlights, but many of them didn't. So there were some dark blocks within my journey. Even though I was afraid of being alone in the dark in our basement at home, I thought it was neat walking in the dark outside. Being out after dark and on my own made me feel more grown. What's more, I had Mom and Dad's permission to be out after dark since there was a need for it, which was to get home after practice.

Every day, Mom served dinner when Dad got home from work at five o'clock sharp. Dinnertime lasted until the last plate was cleaned and placed back in the cupboard. Depending on the vegetable of the day, dinnertime could last well over an hour. Dishwashing didn't start until the last plate was empty. My brother and I sometimes sat alone together at the table, defiantly staring at our vegetables and at each other after Mom, Dad, and Sue had retired to the living room to watch television. A prank I enjoyed pulling on Brett was telling him that kids his age could get sick if they ate the vegetables all mixed together. Once, while he was separating his peas, corn, and carrots, Mom returned to the kitchen and scolded him for playing with his food instead of eating it. When he tried to explain that I had told him it was necessary to do so that he wouldn't get sick, she didn't want to hear his nonsense. She probably thought he was making it up. He fell for pranks like that often. When we finally cleaned our plates, having eaten the last morsels of vegetables, which had turned cold over an hour ago, Sue and I would do the dishes.

Doing dishes seemed to take forever, but it really only took about fifteen minutes. We'd switch off. One night I'd wash and she'd dry. The next night, she'd wash and I'd dry. We both hated to dry because it was so hard to get those drying towels down to the bottom of the milk glasses. I also hated drying because the one who dried would be the last one finished. On the nights when we had too much homework, though, Mom would excuse us from doing the dishes. When we had activities to rush off to, we could leave before we had finished the dishes, too. Even though I hated doing dishes, I knew I was luckier than the kids who had to do more chores than I had to do at home. Besides making my bed in the morning and taking the garbage out to the curb on Sunday evenings, doing dishes was the only regular job my parents made me do.

Another activity my parents had me involved in was Cub Scouts. Every Monday, I had to go to the Cub Scout meetings over at the school with Dad. I didn't like a lot of the boys in Scouts because they were bullies. I didn't care for some of the things we did at the meetings, either. Even though I learned a lot when we went camping,

I hated it. Except for the camping, though, I never complained about Scouts because I could tell how much Dad enjoyed it. It would have been hard for him to keep going to the meetings if I quit, I figured, because every father there had a son in the Scout troop.

Every Wednesday, my sister and I went to our church, Grace United Methodist Church, on the west side of Joliet along Larkin Avenue. There, we played games with Reverend Chukur. At least, I think he was the minister at that time. Our church has had many ministers through the years. Anyway, the activity we attended with other Sunday school classmates was called MYF, which stood for Methodist Youth Fellowship. The games we played were just for fun, nothing academic. The refreshments, usually Hawaiian fruit punch and big chocolate chip cookies, were good, too. Sometimes I was tricked by biting into a raisin cookie instead of chocolate chip, and I would spit it into a napkin and head to the garbage basket with it. I always have hated raisins. In spite of surprise raisins, attending our church's Youth Group was often my favorite part of the week. At these gatherings, I found myself being more outgoing and more the person I really wanted to be. I acted differently around these kids and the Reverend than I did around the kids in school. I did it because I knew I wouldn't have to perform all the time for them. Since I would only be with these people for an hour-and-a-half on Wednesdays and an hour or so on Sundays in Sunday school, I could be a different person without any problem. If I had to see these people every day for many hours, like the kids at school, I'm sure I would have been the shy guy that I usually was at school. I figured, too, that these kids would be nice to me since we were at church every time we were together. Who would dare make fun of me or call me names in church like some students at school did? Whatever the reason, all of the church kids were nice to me, and they seemed to like me. I liked them, too.

On Thursday, Sue and I had our weekly clarinet lessons. These lessons sometimes made me feel guilty since they cost Dad two dollars, and I rarely practiced for them. Other than band practice, I usually only found time to take my clarinet out of its case on weekend afternoons and occasionally during weekday evenings when I was done with my homework. When I did take my clarinet out of its case at home and play it in the basement, I rarely practiced. Instead of playing my lesson pages from the clarinet book or my band music, I played melodies that I had made up. Then I sometimes wrote my original melodies on the five-lined staff I had written on a blank sheet of drawing paper. Usually, I would need many staves, which were five horizontal lines with four spaces between them on which I would write the music notes. Just in case anyone was listening from upstairs, every ten minutes or so I would play a scale so that it would sound like I was practicing. I didn't want Dad, who had an ear for music, to ask Mom, "What's he doing down there, hon? That doesn't sound like a lesson book." Whether my songs were good or bad wasn't the point. No matter how great the songs may have been, I was too shy to share this secretive part of myself with anyone, not even the family yet. In addition, aside from my shyness, I found the writing of songs to be a very personal experience, like writing in a diary. So, until I was willing to share my songs, the creations were only for me.

I'd get so involved with writing my own melodies that I'd usually lose track of time and still be in the basement when Mom would call down the stairs, "Scott, your lip is going to get too sore again. You've been at it long enough." When I played too long at one sitting, my lower lip would get so sore that I would hardly be able to stand the pain when I'd have to play at the next band rehearsal or event.

As I put my clarinet away, I would put my new melody in the torn lining of my clarinet case. Then I would wash the side of my left hand with my saliva that I'd put in my right palm. Being left handed, everyone always knew when I was writing a lot because I would have gray lead from the pencil smeared all along the left side of my left hand. Anyway, I would leave the song I had written in the lining of the clarinet case until the next time I would find time to do my so-called practicing again. The next time, I'd play the song a couple of times, rip it up into small pieces if I didn't care for it, throw it away, and start writing a new one. I think I started this habit of writing my own music, instead of practicing my lessons, when I was in the third grade.

I started playing the clarinet during the winter when I was in second grade, I believe. The band director, Mr. Mattei, bent his own rules and let me start band earlier than third grade, which was his age requirement. I pestered Mom to let me join because I had this tremendous urge to make music like Sue could. The only difference was that I wanted a trumpet instead of a clarinet. I don't know exactly what logic Mom used on Mr. Mattei to get me in the band at such a young age, but she always seemed to have a way of getting what I wanted if she agreed that I should have it. She probably told him that she wanted me to walk to school with Sue in the morning, and therefore I would be sitting there in the gym every morning anyway. I don't know.

The only problem with joining band near the last half of the school year was that there weren't many instruments to choose from in the band's storage closet. I remember how Mr. Mattei unlocked the door to the long, dark, and damp room in the basement of the school and said, "Leave the door wide open because the light's probably still out." He reached up to the metal chain hanging from the light bulb's fixture on the ceiling and pulled it. Then he said, "Yep, it's still not replaced, but we've got enough light to see." As he looked over several shelves that were nearly empty, he said, "So, Pauls, your mother says you want to be the next Louis Armstrong." I didn't know who Louis Armstrong was, but I shyly agreed with him by nodding my head. I guess he called me Pauls because he didn't remember my first name. He must have forgotten my last name, too. Yet, I was too shy and polite to correct him. Since Paulson and Pauls are close, I probably would have let his error go without mentioning it even if I wasn't shy and polite. Except for Mom and Dad, I always found it difficult to correct mistakes made by adults. I figured that they weren't supposed to make mistakes, and it would be embarrassing for them to find out a kid had caught their mistakes. Since calling me a wrong name wasn't important at the time, I let it slide. I then couldn't help but wonder if he thought Mom and Sue's last name was Pauls, too. Again, it didn't matter at the time.

From the doorway of the band storage closet where I was standing, I only could see some rusty snare drums, a tuba, and huge cobwebs. With those choices, I was starting to think that I really wouldn't want to join until a trumpet was available for me, maybe at the beginning of the next school year. The tuba was too big for me and I didn't want to be one of those drummers who made more noise than music, in my humble opinion. Eventually, when I started liking rock and roll music in future years, I developed a higher opinion of drummers. Mr. Mattei said, "I've got more drummers than I need." I was glad to hear that. Then he said what I already realized by saying, "The tuba's too big for a little guy like you, Pauls." Then he finally said, "Since I don't have a trumpet, let's see how you do with this." He reached way up to the top shelf, which was a good stretch for him since he was short, and brought down a long, skinny black case, which I hadn't been able to see from where I was standing due to my lack of height. At the time, I was only seven years old and wasn't very tall yet. Mr. Mattei dusted the case off with his hand and popped the lid open. I was surprised to see that it was a clarinet. I knew what a clarinet looked and sounded like because that's what my sister played in the band. This clarinet, however, wasn't black or in five pieces which would need to be put together before playing it. It was only in two pieces. There was a long, silver metal part and a small black plastic mouthpiece, which Mr. Mattei assembled. He took a clarinet reed out of his suit coat pocket, wet it in his mouth, and put it on the underside of the mouthpiece. Then he started playing notes up and down the scale real fast. He played the clarinet very well and very, very loud. He sounded much better than what I heard come out of a clarinet when Sue played.

Then he handed me the clarinet, and it was love at first sight. He told me how to form my mouth, rolling my lower lip over my bottom teeth and putting my upper front teeth on the top of the black mouthpiece. He then instructed me to blow into the clarinet's mouthpiece to make the reed vibrate, which he further explained, would produce the sound. He was very thorough in his instructions, which I appreciated. I wanted to do this right. After making one ear-piercing squeak, Mr. Mattei told me to keep my cheeks in and not balloon them out when I blew into the mouthpiece. With this instruction, I tried again and failed. Then he grabbed my two cheeks with one hand and said, "Try to keep them in." At that, I played my first note. The note I played was a G since I didn't have any of the holes covered or any keys pressed.

About a year later, during third grade, this antique clarinet was replaced with a black, wooden clarinet like my sister's and the other clarinet players' clarinets. When I got the newer clarinet, I discovered that I could play well. With a newer clarinet, which was probably left behind by someone who quit the band, Mr. Mattei discovered I could play as well as some of the older kids, too, because that is when he moved me up from the third row to the first row in the band's clarinet section.

At the beginning of fifth grade, Mom and Dad sent Sue and me to a new teacher for our clarinet lessons. I was sometimes a little nervous because, as I mentioned before, sometimes I hadn't even looked at the pages of music I'd be playing for my clarinet teacher. Mom told me that the new teacher, Mr. Williamson, was a professional musician. He taught at a music shop in downtown Joliet. She advised that this teacher was much older than the young guy who had been teaching us before in our neighborhood. Mr. Williamson was said to be very good and didn't teach much since he made money playing the clarinet in public. Yet, he taught a couple nights a week.

Mr. Mattei had a music shop of his own and also gave music lessons. I never knew why I didn't go to him for the lessons. He probably charged more than the two dollars Mr. Williamson charged. I'm not sure. Even though I didn't often practice the pages Mr. Williamson had assigned, I always managed to get through my lesson respectfully, I guess. He would have been very impressed if he had known I was sight-reading for him many times. I never told him. If I had told him, he would have thought it was rotten that I was wasting two bucks of my Dad's hard-earned money every week just to play for him while not practicing the clarinet book to become a better player. Then again, maybe he was used to his students not preparing for their lessons. After all, I hardly ever heard Sue play anything at home, let alone the clarinet lesson book.

During my lessons, sometimes Mr. Williamson would grab his clarinet, turn away so I couldn't see his fingers on his clarinet and he would play a note. Then I would play the same note on my clarinet. Eventually, he started playing several notes, and I would echo what he had played, note for note. He seemed to get a kick out of doing that. I only liked doing it because it helped pass the half hour quicker. He also liked to talk about the popular songs and to get my opinion on which ones I thought were good. Occasionally, there were lessons where I hardly played anything in the music book or played any of my band music at all. Those weeks were all right with me, too. When my lesson ended every week, I would run over to Polk Brothers, a nearby store, and go to the record section and look at the 45-rpm record disk covers. Sometimes I counted to see how many records were there, of my favorites, figuring that if there weren't many, it was probably selling well. I usually didn't have money to buy any, but I made a mental note of which one I'd buy next week if I had the sixty-nine cents plus a couple cents tax to buy one in the future. In addition, I would get three record surveys, which were located by the rack displaying the single records. I would get one for myself, one for my dad, and one for Mr. Williamson since they both liked music, probably as much as I did. Even though Sue liked listening to songs on the radio, she wasn't interested in the record charts. Then I would go back to the music shop and would look at the music books and supplies in the front room of the music store while waiting for my sister's lesson to end. When Sue's lesson ended, Dad would pull up in front of the music shop to take us home. Mr. Williamson would follow us out to the car almost every week. He would tell Dad that Sue needed to practice more. I don't remember him ever saying that I needed to practice more, though I am sure there were some weeks he felt I should have.

If Dad didn't give us the money to pay Mr. Williamson while we were in the music shop, Dad would take out his wallet and pay him. Many weeks, seeing Mr. Williamson get paid felt weird to me. After all, he seemed to have a much better time than I did at these lessons. Yet he was the one getting paid for our time together. Go figure. Before heading home with Dad and Sue, I would give Mr. Williamson his copy of the record survey.

Driving home, I would convince myself to practice the pages that Mr. Williamson had assigned me in the lesson book before my next Thursday's lesson. That way, I wouldn't be nervous when I'd play for him again. Also, my luck might run out as far as being able to play the lessons well without practicing ahead of time. After all, the further I was getting in the clarinet skills' book, the more difficult the pages of music were becoming. With nearly every passing page, there were more notes on the page including more notes within one measure. This meant I would be playing more notes. Some lessons were in difficult keys as well, which meant that I had to play more notes that were flat and sharp rather than mostly natural notes. Anyway, if I were to practice for the next lesson, I wouldn't feel guilty about seeing Dad hand Mr. Williamson his money. As Mom used to tell Sue and me, we certainly didn't deserve the ride downtown and the costly music lessons if we didn't practice.

Yet, I found it difficult to fight my urge to create my own music rather than to practice my lessons, which was obviously music someone else had written. Though I thought the constant desire to write was kind of odd, I knew I could stop if I really wanted to or had to do so. Through all of this, however, I never considered quitting the lessons because taking music lessons was something kids in the band were supposed to do. Well, maybe the drummers didn't. I don't know about them. However, everyone else in the band who actually made music was supposed to take music lessons.

Maybe I should have suggested to Mom and Dad that I quit the lessons. No, I probably would have dropped the thought. By not wanting to take music lessons, I might have disappointed them. If there was one thing that I was terrified of doing, it was disappointing Mom and Dad. Though I don't think they meant to, they always looked so disappointed when I did something unpleasant. Dad, especially, couldn't hide the look of disappointment when I didn't come through for him. He probably looked sad mostly because he felt sorry for me when I messed up. However, it looked like he was disappointed at those times, too, and it was very difficult for me to see him that way. I felt the same when my brother or sister disappointed Dad. No matter who caused his disappointment, I hated to see him unhappy. Both Dad and Mom tried real hard to make us three kids turn out right, and they didn't deserve to see us mess up. Not wanting to see Mom mad and not wanting to see Dad unhappy were the reasons why I tried to please them as often as possible.

Other weekly activities included bowling league on Saturday mornings during the winter months of the school year. Though I liked the kids who were on the same bowling league as I was during fifth grade, I got frustrated on the Saturdays when I couldn't get the bowling ball to go where I wanted it to go. This particular season, that happened quite a few Saturday mornings. It wasn't that I got many gutter balls, but I sure didn't get many strikes or spares. Sometimes, I couldn't get any strikes or spares, and I would get so mad at myself. It would have been worse, I'm sure, if kids in my class had seen me bowl so poorly. However, except for a couple of the drummers from the school band, no other bowlers were from my school.

Boxing class over at the school during the winter months was on Saturday mornings. Mom was afraid that I'd get hurt in boxing, so being allowed to go to boxing was Dad's doing. I wanted to try this and enjoyed it. Being the only left-handed boxer in the entire class of about a dozen guys, the instructor put me at the far right end of the long line of boxers. He told me to do everything just the opposite of what he'd tell all the other boys to do, punch-wise and foot-wise. This was confusing for me. I'm sure I would have been confused enough if I was right-handed like the instructor and the other students because most of the time I was lousy at anything to do with sports. However, I really wanted to do this. Due to my lack of boxing ability and due to my confusion from being the only left-handed boy there, Mom was definitely right. I went home sore, after having taken it on the chin, many Saturdays. The Saturday that I came home after having taken it on the eye instead of the chin, Mom insisted that I quit. She got that disappointed look from Dad but there were no arguments from me. Though I had always had aqua blue eyes, this was my first black and blue eye. Embarrassed with the bruised eye, I stayed out of my parents' conversation about my future, or lack of future, in the boxing world. I didn't like how it felt and absolutely hated how it looked in the mirror. I prayed extra hard that night that it wouldn't show by morning. I would have been extremely embarrassed to go to Sunday school with it. Worse yet, I wouldn't want to go back to school with it on Monday. Even though it faded a little more every day, the bruise showed for several days. Nobody said a word about my black eye at church or at school except for a girl named Bonnie who sat next to me in band. It was the first time she had initiated a conversation so far this school year as she only spoke to me when there was something wrong with me that she wanted to point out to me. The first thing she did when I sat down at band practice next to her that Monday was to say, "You've got a black eye." I said, "I know." That was it. In this instance, like so many others, I found that some of the things I worried about never gave me much of a problem at all. I was so sure that people would question me about the black eye and then might laugh at me or tease me for having it. They didn't.

Chapter Five: Sundays

I loved Sundays! My family was always busy on this day. We went to church in the morning. Sue, Brett, and I would go to Sunday school in the big, new, brick church that had just opened up on the West Side of Joliet recently. Before that, we attended an old, wooden, white church, which was in Joliet's old neighborhood, as Mom called it. Both churches were on the West Side, but the new one was further west in a neighborhood with newer homes and some businesses nearby. Like at the old church, Mom would sit in church while Dad would usher the people to the pews and then later pass the collection plate. When Dad wasn't busy helping out, he would sit in the pews with Mom. We kids sat with them in church during summers when Sunday school was on summer break. I enjoyed Sunday school pretty much, but the hour or more in church seemed long because my mind would drift when the preacher seemed to be talking for the benefit of the adults more than children. The good part of the service is when Dad would be with us in the pews and sing the hymns with us. He sang the songs loud and proud, and I always looked forward to hearing him sing in church. Nobody sang the short hymn of praise to the Lord, *Doxology*, as robust as my dad. I got chills all over every time I heard him sing it, and it was part of the church service every Sunday.

Afterwards, we would go out to eat, far from home, so that we could enjoy the ride, too. During our long rides, Mom and Dad were like tour guides, pointing out anything they thought we'd like to see and anything they thought we'd learn from seeing. Mom often said that she would have liked to be a teacher if she had had the education to become one. To me, she was a teacher almost every day anyway, teaching me something.

When the ride to and from the restaurant was exceptionally long, we'd look for as many out-of-state license plates on cars and trucks as we could find. Naturally, most of the plates we saw were from our state of Illinois. When we spotted another state's license, it was cause for a small celebration. Brett and I would cheer as Sue would write it down on a list in a notebook. If it was a plate we had never seen, she would also write down its colors. Illinois plates were easy to spot because they were distinctive with gold lettering on a royal blue base. On the top of the license, it said 19 Illinois 60. Under the license plate's big bold numbers in the middle of the plate, which had up to seven digits to it, it said Land of Lincoln. Illinois first started putting the words Land of Lincoln, named after Abraham Lincoln who was a former United States president, on the license plates in 1954. Other states' licenses were different colors. Sue created the game and seemed to be the quickest at spotting any license from a state other than Illinois.

After eating lunch out, we would go home for a while. Then on most Sundays, we would end up visiting Grandma at her house for a time. Also, we would go to the church's MYF if Reverend Chukur had anything planned for that particular late afternoon. If our visit to Grandma's house was short or if we didn't have an MYF activity, I would take my clarinet down in the basement to do my kind of practicing again. In other words, I'd write music. Hearing the huge church organ through the walls of our Sunday school class was a great inspiration for me to write my own songs. I loved the massive sound of the church's organ.

Before six o'clock, I would try to have homework completed. If it was finished, I could watch television with the family. Besides Saturday night's *Bonanza*, the only western I liked of the many westerns on television during those days, and *The Lawrence Welk Show*, the music show with which Dad would always sing or whistle along, Sunday evening was the best time for watching television all week.

Timmy and Lassie came on first. It was an interesting show about a boy named Timmy and his dog, Lassie. After that show, we would leave the television set on Channel 2 for *Dennis the Menace* which was a funny show about a young boy named Dennis. He seemed to be such a nice and polite kid, but he always caused grief for himself, his parents, or his neighbor, Mr. Wilson. I think I, as well as every other kid I knew, could relate to Dennis. So many times, kids mean to do well but end up doing something unacceptable in adults' eyes. Another reason I liked this show was because Dennis, with his long hair in front, looked so much like Chuck. In many ways, he was funny like Chuck, too. Later, we would watch *The Ed Sullivan Show*. It was referred to as a variety show because there was a wide variety of entertainers on the program every week. Besides enjoying some of the singers of the biggest and best songs of the day on this show, I liked the comedians who would stand there and tell jokes and the ventriloquists who would stand or sit with their dummy or puppet and have a silly conversation. I enjoyed them a lot, because they always could make me laugh and because I never saw this type of entertainment any other place on television. Besides these entertainers, Mr. Sullivan had dancers and other types of entertainers on his show. What was unusual was that Mr. Sullivan never entertained. No, I shouldn't say that. It was somewhat entertaining just to watch him introduce the acts. What I mean is that Mr. Sullivan didn't have an act like telling jokes or singing or doing anything else. Yet it was funny to see him on stage with his stiff neck and awkward movements as he'd clasp his hands like he was nervous when he spoke to the audience and the television camera. At the beginning of the show, he usually said something like, "Tonight, ladies and gentlemen, we have a really big shoe for you." He meant to say that he had a really big show for us, but he had an accent that made it sound like he had a really big shoe instead of a show. At first, I thought he could have been doing it on purpose to be funny. However, after a while, I realized that this guy wasn't trying to be funny at all. It was just how the man actually talked.

Then, we would switch to Channel 5 for the first half of *The Dinah Shore Chevy Show*. It had been Mom's favorite show for a couple of years. Dinah Shore was the type of lady that was popular with mothers, I guess. Dinah would show her big teeth as she laughed heartily from her toes on up. I used to silently joke that Dinah Shore looked like a dinosaur. Dinah Shore and dinosaur, get it? Unless Mom insisted we keep Dinah's show on, we would go back to

Channel 2 after a half-an-hour, at 8:30, for the riotously funny show called *The Jack Benny Program*, which was on from 8:30 to 9:00. Unlike *Dennis the Menace*, which appeared to be designed to make kids laugh, *The Jack Benny Program* made everybody laugh. The situations Mr. Benny got himself into were always hysterical. The funniest part of the show to me was when he talked to a sarcastic, funny black man named Rochester on the show. Sometimes Rochester had a way of getting Mr. Benny to look rather unintelligent and to make everybody laugh in the process. At nine o'clock, we watched the hilarious *Candid Camera* program. Allen Funt, the name of the show's creator and moderator, had a hidden camera and showed films of people who would be caught in awkward circumstances. The circumstances were usually very uncomfortable situations for the people who were being caught on camera by Mr. Funt. Though I usually felt sorry for the people getting trapped in one of his pranks, I couldn't help but laugh at the people's reactions to the situations in which they were trapped. People's reactions to the frustrating situations made the show a huge success with me. This show taught me that people could sure be funny when they are just being themselves. My family always laughed a lot during this show. Sunday nights were probably the only time all week that I couldn't help but laugh out loud. It's something shy people don't ordinarily do.

If Mom and Dad were in an exceptionally good mood, and they usually were after *Candid Camera*, the three of us kids could all stay up for the game show, *What's My Line?* It was a panel game show, which means it had a group of people who would interact with a guest. Four people on the panel would ask a person different questions and try to figure out what kind of job they had, or what line of work they did to make money. I always thought the show should have been called "What's My Line of Work?" Anyway, at the end of the show, which was the best part of the show in my opinion, the four panelists would put blind folds on. Then a famous person came out on stage and the four panelists would ask questions that could only be answered yes or no. The famous person would sometimes disguise his or her voice so that it would be more difficult for the panelists to guess who he or she was. Even though the object of the game was to stump the panelists, I always felt sorry for the famous people who stumped the panel. After all, if they were famous, they would want everyone, even four blindfolded television show panelists, to know them. By the end of this show, the whole family would be tired and head to bed. After a terrific day with the family on Sundays, it's no wonder that I didn't like having to go to bed. In addition, I really didn't like having to go to school the next morning. I wished it could have been Sundays with the family every day, forever.

Chapter Six: The End of the First Grading Period

After seven weeks of school, the first report card of the new school year came out. Actually, the grading period ended after six weeks, but we always got our report cards the Friday after the grading period ended. Throughout the entire school year, we had six grading periods that lasted six weeks long. This time, the only grades on my report card were either A or B. That was good enough to keep me in the "A" row, but I fell back one seat to the fourth seat in the first row. My friend Ray moved from the "D" row to two seats ahead of me. The day Miss McCauley assigned our new seats for the new grading period, many students were talking about Ray's huge upward move as it was an unexpected surprise. When Miss McCauley assigned new seats, it was the first time she called Ray the name everybody else called him. Before then, she had been calling him by his real name, Raymond. Our teacher was finally starting to use his nickname, too.

At recess, the rumor was that Ray's mother had come over to the school at the beginning of the school year and complained to the principal about Ray's last row seat. I didn't want to believe that a mother's complaint could have that much, if any, influence on a report card average. But it appeared as though it did. How could anyone practically be an idiot as determined by his fourth grade report card average and then be a near-genius after the first six weeks of fifth grade? It didn't add up.

I never said a word to Ray about the rumors. What good could it possibly have done? Besides, being a friend of mine, I was glad he sat closer to me and that he didn't look like a dunce anymore by sitting over in the "D" row. Naturally, I would have preferred that he was two seats behind me instead of two seats in front of me. Regardless, even though he had a silly looking smile that made him look like he wasn't very intelligent, I suppose it was nice to see it again. As far as I could see, he never smiled over in the "D" row.

In the shuffle of seats, I still sat near Chuck who was still in the "B" row. So, both Ray and Chuck sat really close to me. Having figured when Miss McCauley would likely fall asleep behind her newspaper most every day, around 1:45 or so, the three of us started passing notes to one another. Before this year, I thought that passing notes was only for girls. I learned, however, that in a class where no one was allowed to talk, writing notes and passing them became a necessity for both girls and boys. While many girls were often afraid of some of the teachers, even boys feared Miss McCauley. Perhaps that is why the girls always passed notes in the earlier grades. Before this year, I never passed a note. I would just whisper to some kid that I needed to talk to, even though I didn't do it often. This year, the kids who whispered or talked during class got Miss McCauley's evil eye as she sharply snapped, "Shhh!" Then she added something like, "Keep quiet or you'll be spending some time with me during recess and lunch hour." Other teachers threatened to send bad kids to the office. Miss McCauley never did. She knew we feared her much more than Principal Monge, and therefore she kept him out of her disciplinary threats.

Speaking of Miss McCauley falling asleep, I always felt sorry for her when she would start to snore. The kids would snicker and she would wake up startled. Her plump body looked like it was trying to jump out of the chair, and I thought that one day she might even fall over as she was quickly trying to get up. Her newspaper would make a crumpling sound as it got all wrinkled up from her own commotion. The kids would briefly laugh, including me. I couldn't help it. It was such a foolish thing to see. In spite of herself, I liked her. I really think she liked me, too. When I was frustrated by something I couldn't figure out quickly in our work, I would raise my hand and patiently wait until she'd notice me. When she would call on me, I would walk up to her right side since that was the closest side of her from where I sat. When I would show her what I couldn't figure out, she would turn to the page where I would find the answer. She would tap the paragraph where the answer was and say, "Read this." She always guided me the right way, and I guess that is all she should have done. If she had just given me the answers over and over again, there would be no sense in doing the work because I probably wouldn't have learned much at all that way.

Some students rarely asked her anything. I didn't think it was because all of them could find all the answers themselves. It was most likely because they were too afraid of her and didn't want to have to stand next to her. Two years ago, if Sue didn't do well in Miss McCauley's class, maybe it was because she was a student who rarely dealt with the teacher. I dealt with Miss McCauley because I wanted her to know that I wanted to learn. More than that, I wanted to learn how to read and write as well as any adult could. I didn't want to end up like the poor, hungry bums on Skid Row who Mom had told me about. As much as Mom knew about Skid Row, I assumed that it was in Joliet.

When I got curious enough about Skid Row and looked it up in a book at school, I was surprised to read that it was a well-known section of Chicago and some other large cities as well. Skid Row was the name of an area in some big cities where poor people gathered, set up outdoor camp, and lived together. The one nearest to where I lived was on the West Side of Chicago on Madison Street. When I told Mom and Dad what I had read, I asked if we could take a ride through it one day. Dad said he had driven through it before and it was interesting to see. Mom said that maybe we could but was concerned about how safe the area would be. I knew we wouldn't have to be scared there, not since Dad would be with us. I always figured bums were in the situation they were in because they failed in school and didn't learn enough to keep a decent job. Being a fifth grader, I may have been kind of young to worry about my future, but in that way I guess I was different. Mom must have thought that talking about Skid Row in front of us kids would motivate us to do our schoolwork at times. I don't think she was trying to scare us. More than anything, her references to the Skid Row bums made me curious. I really wanted to see the place.

At home, everything was gradually getting settled again. Mom was starting to act more like her old self, occasionally asking if I had homework and wondering how I was doing in school. As long as my report card was all right, I wasn't hearing any complaints about Miss McCauley. My mom was the type of parent that would wonder what was wrong with the teacher if I got a bad grade. I knew, of course, that the only time I usually got a grade lower than a B was when I wasn't working on the subject hard enough. The times I tried to tell my mom that I was the problem and the teacher wasn't, she probably didn't want to believe me.

Like in third grade, I got my first grade lower than an A. I think I got a C in history that year. Even though I didn't do all the work because I didn't like the book, my mom marched over to the school and criticized the teacher for being too young and inexperienced to teach. I guess that's one big reason I always tried to keep my grades up. If I didn't get a good grade, Mom would blame the teacher. All the while, the teacher and I would know whose fault the lower grade probably was. The fault would more often than not be my own.

I remember last year in fourth grade, my teacher whose name was Mrs. Lindsay made me take a test paper home to get it signed. It was a history test with a D written big in red ink on the top of the page. Mrs. Lindsay was disgusted with many of the students in the class for doing poorly on the test, and she decided to punish us by making us show our parents our grades. Well, Mom signed it and put it in a sealed envelope. When I took it back to school, the teacher asked, "Did you read what your mother wrote?" Surprised that she wrote anything more than her name, I emphatically said, "No!" I thought my mother had just signed it and put it in the envelope for safekeeping for me. From Mrs. Lindsay's tone of voice and hand-on-hip stance with raised eyebrows, I sensed that she might not believe that I hadn't read the note. But she said, "All right, come with me." She walked to her file cabinet, opened the second drawer from the top, which was labeled History. Took out another copy of the history test I had done poorly on the day before, and took me down the hall to a seventh grade classroom. She whispered something to the seventh grade teacher, probably telling him that she wanted me to sit in there for a short time. Mrs. Lindsay told me to sit at a vacant desk and take the test again.

I broke out into a cold sweat. It must have been that Mom wrote Mrs. Lindsay a note saying that I could do better on the test if I was given a second chance. Mom probably told her to let me try the test again. The truth was that I didn't know any more about the history lesson this particular day than I did the day before. But what could I do? I just sat there with this classroom of seventh graders and started taking the test again as Mrs. Lindsay left the room. After about ten minutes or so, Mrs. Lindsay came back, leaned over my shoulder, and looked at my paper. She didn't look happy but didn't look surprised either. As she pointed to one of my answers, she asked, "Is this what you think the answer is?" Embarrassed, I said nothing. She finally said, "OK. Let's go back to our room." She never said another word about the note or the test. Mom didn't either. Maybe I should have told Mom and Dad that they were expecting too much from me at times. Or maybe, more accurately, I should have told them that they were expecting more than I sometimes gave of myself. But I would have disappointed them by saying that, and I just couldn't do it. Therefore, I would just have to make myself try harder whether I liked the subject or not.

The day Miss McCauley assigned our new seats, I dreaded telling Mom that I fell back one chair in the class's "A" row. But when I told her after school, all she said was, "That's okay. You'll be first next time." Little did she know that I had no hopes or desires of ever being number one. I just felt fortunate to be where I was. After all, this was my schoolwork, not my music. If I could go the rest of the school year in this "A" row, I would have felt very fortunate indeed. I certainly didn't want my mom to have her hopes of me ever being the smartest kid in the class because I sure didn't think I was the smartest. Furthermore, I really didn't care that I wasn't. After all, when you reach the top in academics, you have to work extra hard to stay there. I wouldn't have to work quite as hard to stay there if I never got there. In band, I would love to be the first clarinetist because I wouldn't mind working my fingers and lips off to stay on top. Playing music didn't seem like work to me, anyway. Academic school work did.

In Miss McCauley's class, John was the proudest kid as well as the most miserable. He was the first kid in the "A" row for a second consecutive grading period. All he did was work. He even skipped recess sometimes to sit alone in the classroom in that first seat to stay ahead of the rest of the class. Myself, I had a life outside of school, which included my time on the playground. The other kids in the class did, too. The biggest contradiction I found in John being the smartest kid in the class was that he was a drummer in the band. Before this, I never thought drummers were very smart. Drummers didn't seem to need to know much about music to be in band. It seemed like they were usually just having fun back in the drum section in band rehearsals while the rest of the students in the band were working at playing the music right. I guess I was wrong about this drummer, though. On the day John joined the band, maybe there was nothing but a rusty drum in Mr. Mattei's creepy storage room.

Chapter Seven: Playing by Ear

As always, the first report card of the new school year meant that Halloween would soon follow. This year, I wasn't looking forward to Halloween like I had other years when I'd get excited about the costumes, trick-or-treating, decorations at school and at home, and the candy I'd receive. Beyond it maybe just being a sign that I was getting older and growing out of the activities, I dreaded the coming of Halloween this year. Though I had never given much thought to the morbid and ghostly part of Halloween night in the past, I was thinking about the creepy celebration of death, ghosts, and goblins this year. I knew why I was concentrating on the unpleasant parts of Halloween, too. It was because of Grandpa's death.

Since Grandpa was the first person close to me that had ever died, it's the first time that I saw Halloween in this new and unpleasant way. I couldn't wait for the day to pass so that I wouldn't have to face deadly topics again for a while. I just knew Grandpa's ghost would be on my mind throughout the whole haunted day. For the first time, I had a personal interest in ghosts, particularly Grandpa's ghost, and it caused me to want no part of Halloween. The day was now too scary for me, I guess. If I could have made sense of it, ghosts and all, I suppose I could have managed it. However, I could not comprehend it. Maybe I never would understand it. I wanted to ignore it. Of course, it was hard to ignore something that was on most every doorstep that I passed on my way to and from school, as well as beginning to appear in every hallway and classroom at school. Whether I liked it or not, Halloween was on its way.

The day before Halloween was on a Sunday. This particular Sunday afternoon, we got home from eating out at a restaurant around 2:30 in the afternoon. Since there was no church Youth Group and there was lots of homework to do, Sue and I were at home alone while Mom, Dad, and Brett went to visit Grandma. For a while, I laid in my bed trying to read a book for a book report at school. I couldn't concentrate for three reasons. First, Sue was in her bedroom listening to her transistor radio while she was supposedly doing her homework, and I was concentrating more on what was coming out of her radio and through the wall than my boring book. Secondly, the book I chose from the library to do my report on was turning out to be worse than just boring to me. It was turning out to be the worst book I had picked in recent times. My obsession with dreading Halloween was cluttering my mind, too. Incidentally, the book I picked to read for my book report got good reviews, according to my teacher, but I discovered it was historical after I had taken it home and started reading it. As I mentioned before, I wasn't into history books at all. This one was called *The Witch of Blackbird Pond* by Elizabeth George Speare. It had a recent copyright date of 1957. That was one reason I initially thought it might be good because it wasn't one of those books written a long time ago. However, I should have read about the author before I checked the book out, but I didn't. A description of her said that she wrote historical fiction. I obviously needed to start taking more time in selecting a book when I had to do a report so that the assignment, especially the lengthy reading part, wouldn't be so boring to me. Imagine me, a person who dreaded the coming of Halloween, picking a book with the word witch in the title. What was I thinking?

As I continually tried to read this book, I found myself concentrating more on the music coming from my sister's radio than the content of the book. In my opinion, some of the songs coming out of her radio weren't much better than the school's band music or the music I had to play at my music lessons. Yet, I liked most of the songs. I could recognize the titles of songs within their lyric because I had been reading the WLS Radio's Silver Dollar Survey intently after picking it up in recent weeks at Polk Brothers after my music lessons on Thursdays. It was the new survey that the store was carrying. By studying the list of the hit songs' titles, I was getting ideas as to what type of title might work for some of my better songs that I had been creating in the basement. Thinking that I would write a hit song for some recording artist someday was a very ambitious thought, but I admit to having had that thought.

I always tried to make myself like the number one song because I would think I was too different from other people if I didn't like the most popular song, which most everyone else must have liked. After all, if a song was number one on the record chart, a lot of people had to have liked it. Honestly, though, I didn't care much for some of the very popular songs. A very popular song over the summer was *Alley-Oop* by the Hollywood Argyles. Beyond being a totally stupid song, in my opinion, the lead singer on the record couldn't sing well. It was a novelty song and kids seemed to love it. I would mentally tune it out every time I heard it come on my sister's radio. I much preferred some songs that didn't do quite as well on the music charts. My favorite throughout the fall and beyond was the hit song without words. It was an instrumental called *Walk – Don't Run* by The Ventures. I just couldn't hear that song enough. I loved it! When it played, I found myself moving my fingers on my thumbs, fingering the notes as if I was playing the clarinet. On this particular afternoon, after they finally played *Walk – Don't Run* and started playing Sue's favorite song, *It's Now or Never* by Elvis Presley, I grabbed my clarinet case and headed to the basement. The only singer Sue seemed to like more than Elvis was a guy who was on his parents' television show. His name was Ricky Nelson and his parents' show was called *The Adventures of Ozzie and Harriet*, which is a show that I didn't care for very much. Anyway, I wet my reed and tried playing The Ventures' song on my clarinet, softly. Much like the songs I'd been writing in the basement, this one was fast and had no words. It was my kind of music.

I was very pleased when I realized how easy it was for me to play my favorite song off the radio. Before then, I never previously had tried to do it. Then I started writing the tune out. Since I didn't have the song playing while I was writing the music for it, I couldn't match the key in which the song was played on the radio. This concerned me, but I couldn't do a whole lot about it. To match the key that the song had been recorded, I would have to be hearing the record as I wrote out the music. Since I wasn't hearing it at that time, I just wrote it in a key that worked for me. The song *Walk – Don't*

Run turned out to have only sixteen measures of music, which repeated over and over again. I should say it was that long without the introduction and the drum break. I was pleased in realizing that the songs I'd been creating were usually as long as this hit song. I had previously thought that my songs were way too short to be real songs. Without me knowing it, I must have been playing louder because my sister appeared on the steps to the basement and asked, "Where did you get the music to that?" When I told her I didn't have the music, she seemed confused as she asked, "Scott, you can't play a song without the music, can you?" I just shook my head up and down to let her know that I could.

When Mom, Dad, and Brett got home, Sue brought Mom down in the basement where I was now trying to play other songs I liked and thought I might be able to play. In fact, the current number one and number two songs on the list probably marked the first time in which I liked both of the top two songs a lot. Number one at the time was *Stay* by Maurice White and the Zodiacs and number two was *Save the Last Dance for Me* by a group called the Drifters. The Drifters' song was probably my favorite song on the current chart as *Walk – Don't Run* had already fallen off the weekly chart. I loved the bouncy melody to the Drifters' song. Then I kept listening to hear another song that wasn't being played too much on the radio that I liked. It was a song in which some man sang about men working on the chain gang. That was a great song and I was really hoping it would go to number one. Oddly, I don't think it did very well because I didn't see anything about men working on the chain gang on the record charts when I looked for it. Anyway, I was doing well by playing the catchy parts of these three songs, too. With Mom and now Brett in the basement with Sue, Sue insisted that I play *Walk – Don't Run* for them. I said I didn't want to right then, but Mom coaxed me into playing a little bit of it. I assumed it wasn't Mom's kind of music and she wouldn't care for it. However, she acted as if it was okay. Sue pressed Mom for an answer to the mystery as to how I could play it without the music, Mom said that I was playing by ear. "You know," she continued, "your Grandma could always play the piano by ear, ever since I was a little girl." She said that Grandma didn't know how to read music at all but could play songs real well. I said that it must have been years ago because I never heard Grandma play any musical instrument. Mom said it was long ago when Grandma used to have an old piano in her front room.

Mom asked me about the song, which got Sue so interested in my musical abilities all of a sudden. I told her it was a song I like a lot since it didn't have words, was fast, and had a catchy melody that I couldn't get out of my head. I even liked the title, *Walk – Don't Run*. I liked it because those are the words that were painted in big red letters on the cement next to the swimming pool. Anything that made me think of great times, like going swimming, was a favorite of mine. Also, the title sounds like a rule. I have always liked rules, especially rules that are easy to follow and have an obvious benefit to people. Having sensible rules that people are supposed to follow have always made me feel safe. Therefore, everything about this song, from the music to its title, made it the best song I was hearing on my sister's transistor radio those days.

That evening, as we watched our Sunday night television programs, Sue and Brett excitedly talked about Halloween and how fantastic school would be tomorrow. Mom and Dad talked about whether or not they'd bought enough candy for the trick-or-treaters who would be coming to our door. Rather than buy more candy, they decided they'd give each kid two pennies if they were to run out of candy. During all of this talk, I sat quietly, replacing my fearful thoughts of Halloween with pleasant thoughts of this afternoon's accomplishments on the clarinet, playing my favorite songs. I probably would have skipped a little television and gone downstairs to play the songs again if my lip wasn't already sore from playing the songs so many times that afternoon.

It was nice to see Mom and Dad talking nicely to one another again. They hadn't argued for quite a while. When they first started being nice to one another again, I thought they might have called a truce for the sake of us kids since their arguing made us so sad. But by now, I figured that their arguments had really ended and wouldn't return. They had apparently stopped because they wanted to stop and not because they felt the need to put on a friendly front for us kids. Before we all went to bed, after a real funny half-an-hour of *Candid Camera* and an interesting half-an-hour of *What's My Line?*, Sue asked me if I could play different songs she liked, including *It's Now or Never*. I told her that I'd have to listen to them a lot like I'd listened to *Walk – Don't Run*. Then, I would just have to try it.

Once again, on this night, I was feeling very different. On one hand, I was different in a bad way because I wasn't being enthusiastic about tomorrow's Halloween activities. On the other hand, I was feeling different in a good way because I could play my favorite songs without reading the songs' music sheets. Once again, Sue asked Mom how I could possibly do it. Mom simply said, "It's Scott's gift from God." Mom had talked about God's gifts often. I was very happy to hear that I had a special one.

Chapter Eight: Halloween

The Halloween day I had been dreading for a while was just a couple hours away when I went to bed. I hoped the day would pass quickly for me. Only the nights before Christmas, Easter, New Year's Day, and one's own birthday held more excitement for many people, I guess. Yet, here I was in bed, unable to sleep, as I tried not to think of my first Halloween with Grandpa's soul outside of his body, or as they say, being a ghost. The harder I tried not to think about it, the more I thought about it. The result was then worrying about how I would get through the school day tomorrow if I didn't get enough sleep. If there was ever a prize for the kid who worried the most, I'm sure that I would have won it.

I must have finally fallen asleep around eleven o'clock because I knew it wasn't Halloween yet before I slept. In the morning, when Mom got me up at seven, the first thing I thought about was how many hours would have to pass before the day would be over. Seventeen hours sounded like a long time, but it was better than twenty-four. Of course, the first seven hours of Halloween were easy because I missed them by sleeping. It was too bad that I couldn't have slept all day. As I got ready for school and ate a breakfast of oatmeal and milk, I kept thinking about my last thoughts of the previous night. I was thinking how terribly strange I was to be dreading a day that everybody else couldn't wait to see arrive. If there was just one other person in the whole wide world who hated this Halloween as much as I did, I would have wanted to spend the entire day with that person. Of course, I was sure that no such person existed. Therefore, I dropped the thought and, once again, felt there was something wrong with me. I wanted to tell Mom what I thought of this Halloween, but I was afraid she'd already thought I was different enough. Why should I worry her about this, too? Furthermore, to explain all of this to my mom, I would make her sad by having to mention Grandpa's ghost.

Before I left for school with Sue, along with my lunch box, Mom handed me a brown paper sack, which held a piece of burned cork and one of Dad's old flannel shirts. These were for transforming myself into a hobo for my Halloween party at school. She explained that I should smear the burned cork on my forehead, cheeks, and chin, as well as on the backs of my hands, so I would look like I had a dirty face and hands. Though I had already known about hobos, Mom explained, "Hobos don't wash themselves clean." I told her that I didn't think I'd dress for the party this year. The only reason I admitted to her that I was contemplating going without wearing a costume this year was to get her opinion. As always, she gave it. Though she didn't make a big deal about me not wanting to be in a costume, she said, "You'll probably be the only one without a costume if you don't put it on." She knew that standing out in a crowd bothered me, and I'd probably end up wanting to wear the costume to be like everybody else. For the moment, I compromised by saying that I'd take the costume in the bag to school but couldn't promise to wear it. She simply repeated, "You'll probably be the only one."

After lunch at school, I kept my eyes wide open as the students came out of the washrooms in their costumes. I was looking for just one other kid in my class without one so that I wouldn't feel like I'd have to put mine on. Sure enough, it looked like I'd have to put on my hobo shirt and smear some of the burned cork on my face to look dirty like a real hobo in need of a good bath. But then, Chuck came through for me. I saw him all alone at the end of the hallway and yelled to him, "Aren't you going to put on a costume?" He quietly shook his head to say no. Then he walked over and said, in a soft voice, "Nah, I didn't want to. That's kids' stuff. When are these people gonna grow up, anyway?" I said, "That's what I thought. My mom made me bring a costume, but I told her I wouldn't promise to put it on." Chuck perked up and asked, "So, you're not going to wear one either?" "No," I hesitantly said.

As we went into the classroom, I started to realize that Chuck's comment about fifth graders being too old for costumes was probably phony. If his Mom had given him a costume, I bet he'd be wearing it. Again, I felt myself disliking his mom even though I hardly knew her. Chuck wasn't getting to be a kid at all since his mom wouldn't do her job as a mom, like getting him a costume. Though I may have appeared the same as Chuck that afternoon in the classroom, our reasons for not being in costumes were very different. He needed a good mom so he could do these kids' things, and I needed to be normal. I really felt different. Or, I should say that I felt different until Ray walked over as he was lining up for the costume competition with the others in costumes. He howled, "Lucky you!" As he slipped his wolf's mask on, he continued, "My mom made me bring this stupid thing!" I thought my hobo outfit had a better chance of winning the best costume contest than that mask I'd seen year after year at stores in Joliet, next to the Halloween candy counters.

Winning the Halloween costume contest wasn't important to me anyway since I'd already won it once. I won two years ago in third grade. I remember that Mom had me go home for lunch that day with my sister. Just before I headed back to school, Mom and Sue caught me off guard. "Here, put this on over your other clothes," Sue said as they pulled one of Sue's party dresses over my head. I could see that it was the pink dress with a real big bow on the back. They didn't even give me a chance to see myself in a mirror. They pushed me out the door and then Sue and I headed back to school. Just before we got there, my sister reached in a brown paper bag and pulled out a tiny pink purse she would carry when she had worn the dress. She told me to keep the dress up on my shoulders or it might fall off because I was too big for it and Mom couldn't zip it up in back. Unzipped, it was hanging a little loose on me on top. Her final instruction to me before she headed to her class was to say, "When you line up for the contest in your classroom, Scott, have the purse hanging on your shoulder. It's part of the costume." As she walked away, she turned and said, "And don't lose it. I want it back."

When I walked in the room, everyone roared with laughter. For the first time in a long time, I was the center of attention and didn't mind it. When I was much younger, I didn't mind being the center of attention much. This was like a flashback in time for me. The class's laughing didn't bother me because I knew they were laughing at my costume and not at me. I could see that I was bringing them lots of enjoyment and I liked doing so. When we finally lined up for the teachers from other classrooms to walk in and judge us, the teachers saw me and laughed almost as loud as the kids did when they had first seen me in the dress. Then they talked behind their hands for less than half-a-minute. Then one of them announced, "Mrs. Paulson is the winner!" Everyone laughed and applauded for Sue's dress, the purse, and me. Thinking about my Halloween school day in third grade made me wish for those happier times again. I missed not being so shy and the way I felt about Halloween before Grandpa died.

Since Scouts was cancelled that night for Halloween, I borrowed Ray's idea of only wearing a mask to do some trick-or-treating with Sue and Brett. Mine looked better on me than Ray's did on him because mine was more elastic and fit better over my glasses than his fit over his glasses. Once again, Mom told my sister, brother, and me not to eat any unwrapped candy except for Mrs. Palmer's brownies. With that reminder, we remembered that Mrs. Palmer's brownies were the best treats on Halloween. Therefore, my sister and I decided to head my little brother in the direction of her house first.

The first house we went to had no answer at the door. I thought about soaping their screen on the front door with the small piece of used Ivory soap, which I had wrapped in toilet paper and hidden in my jacket pocket. However, since we were right across the street from our house and the people might really be in there watching, I didn't. Being caught in the act of soaping doors would be bad enough. Being caught by nearby neighbors would be even worse. Having the people across the street know I was doing a criminal act on Halloween wouldn't be good. Yet, I thought that some people just might not answer their doors because they might not like kids or they might not like the idea of handing out candy to kids for nothing in return. There was also a chance that maybe they couldn't afford to give away free candy. Regardless, being good all the time was boring, and Halloween night was my chance to be somewhat bad.

The next house down was the Palmer house. At this house, we never had to yell trick-or-treat or knock on the front door to get Mrs. Palmer slowly moving towards the door with her brownies. She would leave her inside door open so she could see us coming up the sidewalk to her house. The big pieces of square-shaped brownies with lots of powdered sugar on them were always neatly piled high on a huge white doily, which was sitting on a huge silver platter. Halloween evening was practically the only time I had seen her all year except for rarely seeing her in the passenger's seat of the car her husband drove in and out of their garage. She never hung out in her front yard. Maybe because she recognized us as being kids who lived nearby, she always insisted that we take two of her moist chocolatey treats that practically would melt in my mouth. She would carefully put them on some fancy papers, which she would wrap individually around the two pieces, and then she would place them in my hand. I'd eat both of them before we'd get to the next house as I wouldn't want to put them in my candy bag and possibly crush them under the weight of the other candy that I'd be receiving. Mrs. Palmer's brownies were so, so good.

Besides the brownies, I liked how she simply gave us the goods, heard us say thanks, and let us leave. This year, when she gave me mine, she said, "If I remember correctly, you like the brownies with nuts in them." While I was surprised that she must have known that from years past, as I didn't remember us discussing it before, I simply said, "I like them all, Mrs. Palmer." She said, "The two I already gave you have nuts in them." Then she smiled, winked, and added, "And here's one without nuts." The nice neighbor lady gave me three instead of two.

At other houses, a few of our nearby neighbors would come to the door and talk to us. They'd ask, "Aren't you the Paulson children? You kids are getting so big. How's your mother doing? I haven't seen her lately." On occasion, someone would say, "Susie, you look just like your mom." Others would say, "You kids look just like your dad." When I'd hear that, I thought that we kind of looked like both of them. People who lived farther away from us would start a conversation by asking who we were and what block we lived on. I shouldn't have minded talking to people who gave free candy, but the small talk always slowed us down. Sue was always the polite, talkative one. I'd just start walking back down the sidewalk in front of their house with Brett. Besides, I don't think Sue had a shy bone in her body. She would talk to anyone. I was shy. Brett, who was just in kindergarten, was too young to carry on a good conversation with an adult. Regardless of the excuses for not having conversations at the houses, time was candy! I didn't plan on trick-or-treating too much longer. Therefore, time needed to be spent getting candy and not wasted by talking to strangers.

This year, candy-lover or not, I had a new attitude towards Halloween as we were going from house to house. I got bored fast. Maybe I was getting too old for this, or maybe I had built up such negative feelings for this particular Halloween night that I simply didn't want to participate in it. Even though I wanted to get a good-sized bag of candy, I quickly got burned out on the process. Therefore, after I had gotten my bag almost half-full, I had an irresistible urge to abandon Sue with Brett so that I could walk to Ray's house a few blocks away from where we were. I thought he might have finished taking his little sister trick-or-treating by now since it was getting a little later. As far as I could tell, he usually didn't do things very long with her because she cried so much over everything, and he admittedly didn't like her much. I was preparing for my escape from Sue and Brett. After we finished hitting all the houses on the block we were on, I planned to tell them that they could go on without me and I'd see them at home in a while.

At the next house, a man and his wife, who was standing alongside of him, caught me not paying attention as I was holding my opened bag in front of their front door and faces. The man looked down at me and said, "I just told you, young man, you gotta perform a trick. Entertain me and the little woman here before you get the treat." I must have looked confused because he explained, "You kids come saying trick-or-treat. Then none of you do a trick to get your treat." No one ever had taken the trick-or-treat chant seriously. Besides, I think he had it wrong. To me, trick-or-treat meant that he had to give us a treat or we would play a trick on him. That was the reason lots of kids, including me, had a bar of soap in our pockets. Not having a decent trick to do for him, I just closed my bag and turned to walk away. I obviously wasn't going to put soap on his window with him and the little woman, as he called her, standing right there. Then the man said, "Come back here. I just thought I'd ask for some entertainment since you came to get some candy." He then put something in each of our bags without getting entertained. Through all the confusion, I may have even forgotten to thank him. Shame on me, if I forgot.

The incident with this man and his little woman was enough for me to make my move now instead of waiting until we got to the end of the block. I said, "Well, Sue, that last house did it for me. I'm out of here. I'm going to Ray's house." She screeched, "You can't!" From her desperate reaction, I thought she might have had a hidden agenda, too. Perhaps she also had planned on taking off to a friend's house and sticking me with Brett instead. As I walked away, Sue sternly said that I couldn't do this as Brett started yelling at me for leaving. As he usually did when he was confused or unhappy, he started to cry. I stopped for a moment to tell Sue, "You probably want to go to a friend's house, too. Your friends like Brett. Ray hates little kids. So, Brett will be happier staying with you." Besides, Sue would always try to please Brett when he started crying, but I didn't. I figured that nobody needed to cry as often as he did and that most of his fallen tears were phony.

As I finally walked away towards Ray's house, I heard Sue threaten, "Wait until Mom hears about this!" I stopped for a second. Then I remembered that this was the Halloween I had planned to ignore. It was starting to look like I should have. With that thought, I stubbornly kept on walking away with determination at my side. I reached the corner and turned to stay on course to Ray's house. No, I didn't like doing this to Sue, but what I told her was true. If she had plans to meet up with friends, they would accept Brett with open arms. Ray would have probably told me to take Brett back home before he'd go anywhere with me, and that would only make Brett cry more.

When I got to Ray's place, his mom gave me some bits of taffy wrapped in black and orange papers. She tried to give me extras but I said, "No thank you, Mrs. Monday. I don't really like those." Her face dropped as I realized I am often too honest for my own good. I really didn't mean to be rude. I tried to explain that taffy gets stuck in my teeth. She changed the topic by saying that I was just in time because Ray and his little sister had just gotten home from trick-or-treating. She said that he was just about to head over to Murph's house. I was surprised since I didn't even know that Ray and Murph were friends. It made sense that they would know each other, though, because Murph lived right around the corner and down the street, which was less than a block from Ray's house. I didn't know exactly which house Murph lived in, but I knew he lived somewhere in the middle of that block.

When Ray came upstairs from the basement, he didn't seem happy to see me. He bluntly asked in a nasty tone of voice, "What are you doing here?" I said, "Came over to see your ma. What's it to ya?" After that snide remark, I got serious and told him I didn't care for trick-or-treating this year and managed to get away from Sue and Brett to see if he just wanted to hang around for a while. "Your mom said you're going to Murph's," I said, and quickly added. "Let's go." I decided I'd invite myself since I sensed I wasn't welcome to go with him. Ordinarily, I wasn't that forceful, but I really didn't want to go home yet and I definitely didn't want to be without a friend on this particular Halloween night. I could have gone to Chuck's house, but it would take a lot more time to walk way over to his neighborhood. I was always welcome at Chuck's house. But then again, he probably wouldn't be home until real late since his mom probably wouldn't care what time he would get home. Chuck was probably having a great time with his brother Larry by soaping windows in his neighborhood and doing other mischievous things. Larry was a year older than the rest of us but in the fifth grade with us because he flunked once. I think Chuck told me he failed second grade, but it might have been another grade. Anyway, doing those bad things with Chuck and Larry would have been more fun than hanging around with Ray and his unwelcoming attitude. But, there I was.

As the two of us headed down the street, a car slowly drove up to us and some younger school-aged kids were pointing at me through the back car window yelling, "He's the one, mom. He's the one who soaped the car windows." I yelled back, "No, I didn't soap any windows." I remembered walking past the junk car on the street as I walked to Ray's house, but I just walked by it. They must have seen me walk past it, then saw that their windows were soaped, and then came looking for me as they assumed I did it. I swear to God, I didn't! The mom who was at the steering wheel was yelling at me. I just yelled back one more time that I didn't do it and kept walking with Ray. Ray laughed and said, "You did it, didn't you?" I yelled, "No! I didn't!" The car drove up to the corner and made a U-turn. When it came by again, one of the kids yelled, "We know you did it!" Being accused of doing something I did not do really got me mad. However, I wasn't worried about having done something wrong because I didn't do it. Ray then said, "Everybody around here wishes they'd move away. Those kids play in the middle of the street while the parents sit in the front yard. The dad drinks beer right in their front yard. And, those little kids are always so dirty. They all got the cooties. Nobody talks to them." After a pause, he said with disgust, "My ma says they're white trash."

Chapter Nine: Murph

When we got to Murph's house, Murph's parents gave both of us several regular-sized Hershey's chocolate candy bars, not the tiny candy that most houses give out. Probably since they thought we were Murph's friends, they gave each of us several of them. If the type and amount of candy a household gave out on Halloween was any sign of the family's wealth, this family must have had some big bucks. When Murph came out, he was very nice to me. This surprised me since he was one of the rowdy boys at school. He hung around with the bad guys and even had the mean look. His hair was thick, black, and greased back on the sides of his head. If it wasn't for his fuller face, he would have looked an awful lot like the rock and roll singer Elvis Presley. Murph had a big, warm, contagious smile just like Elvis's, too. When I saw his smile, the only response my face could give was a big smile back. Instead of mean, the kid fit my definition of friendly, which is something I wasn't used to when I was with Ray. Beyond friendly, with his looks, I thought he was cool, too. Every time I had seen him at school, he would always be standing as he was now in front of his house. His thumbs were hooked on each of his two front blue jeans' pockets as he was a little hunched over in his stance. In addition, he dressed more like a high school kid than a grade school kid. He was wearing a white tee shirt under his black leather jacket, just like the jacket a motorcycle rider would wear. He wore black boots like a motorcycle rider might wear, too.

Having met him, the bad boy image and his personality didn't match. He was unusually nice to me, shaking my hand and slapping me on my back as he asked, "You're that kid who plays in the band, aren't you?" I couldn't remember ever having met a kid with such adult-like manners. No kid had ever shaken my hand when I had met him before. By the look on Ray's face, I could tell that he didn't like how well Murph was treating me. But, I didn't know why. If I had just introduced Ray to someone, I would be glad if the person treated him this nicely. Standing next to Murph, I could see that he was a bit taller than I was. From a distance in the past, I didn't know he looked so handsome. Like I said, he looked a lot like Elvis Presley and had physical mannerisms like him, too. Up close, he looked even more like Elvis. I asked him what grade he was in. As I had thought, he said he was a sixth grader. I had seen him around the playground during recess at school this year but not before this school year. He stands out in a crowd due to his clean-cut appearance, the clothes he wears, and the way he carries himself. He then told me that he went to a Catholic school in Joliet before his parents put him in Chaney School at the beginning of this school year. He said he liked going to school closer to home. The best thing, he said, was that he could walk to school rather than deal with a crowded bus every day. He also said that the teachers at our school weren't as strict as the nuns he had for teachers at the Catholic school. However, he missed his friends who went there. He said he never got to see them anymore because they lived in different parts of town. Having found a few good friends at Chaney School, he seemed content to be where he was now. When I asked him why his parents made him go to Chaney School instead of the Catholic school, he laughed a hearty laugh and said, "Things weren't working out for me there." Then he got serious and said, "I think the nuns were happy to see me leave." Though I wanted to ask why the nuns would be happy to see him go to another school, I didn't want to make him uncomfortable by asking him. That conversation could wait until another time.

It wasn't surprising that Murph took over as the leader of our group of three. He led us to the school playground. As he walked, Murph and Ray talked about the last time they'd played pool at Murph's house. It sounded like Ray was good at the game. To include me in the conversation, Murph asked if I'd ever shot pool. When I told him I hadn't, he said he'd have me over to show me how sometime. It became difficult for me to know everything the two guys were talking about because Ray was talking exceptionally soft. He apparently didn't want me to hear him or he simply wanted to exclude me from the conversation. When Murph continued to speak, though, he spoke loud enough to make me feel included. Ray was acting strange towards me. Though he'd acted different before, he had never treated me this strangely. He just wasn't the same person I knew when he was around Murph. And what an unlikely friendship it appeared to be between them. Ray was more like me, a quieter guy who had a reputation of being a good kid. At school, Murph didn't hang around with kids like us.

Furthermore, I could see that Ray didn't want me to meet this other side of himself. I wanted to tell him to relax and act any way he wanted to act, but I didn't because it would have embarrassed him if I had said something critical of him in front of Murph. Given the choice to be the kid that Ray always had been with me or the kid he was with Murph at the school's playground on this Halloween night, the kid he was acting like around Murph won out as being the better one. He was talking in a different tone of voice, a little deeper than his usual tone of voice. He was even walking like Murph. Though Ray's imitation of Murph was somewhat irritating and funny to see, it was better than the nerdy way he usually acted. While Murph started suggesting different Halloween activities we could be doing instead of just hanging around, I kept my eyes peeled for the Chaney Saints. The Saints was the high school gang that supposedly hung out near the school late at night. In fact, some of the members of the gang were older than high school kids. However, I guess it was too early for them because I saw no sign of other people while we were there. As Murph talked to us, I couldn't imagine doing some of the wild things he'd suggested, but they all sounded more exciting than just standing around. The only idea we all accepted was turning over all the garbage cans in the schoolyard. When we did it, I could see that the cans were nearly empty anyway which meant we weren't making too much of a mess. Other than being an aggravation to Sam, the school janitor, this prank was harmless. Undoubtedly, Sam would be the one who would have to turn the garbage cans right side up sometime tomorrow during the school day and put the garbage back in the cans. When we went to soap some of the school windows, we found that many bars of soap had already found the windows and had made their marks. So, we walked over to the monkey bars and sat on them for a time.

Monkey bars, initially called a jungle gym, was a metal contraption invented around 1920 for children to get some exercise and to play games outdoors. Thinking we weren't kids anymore, we just sat on them. I hadn't been near the monkey bars since fourth grade. It felt somewhat sad to be getting too tall to play on them comfortably. Though there was hardly anything I liked about being a kid most of the time, I had to admit that it was more fun to hang by my arms from the monkey bars or to hang upside down from them than to just sit like an older kid is expected to do. If I'd started climbing or hanging upside down, Ray surely would have said something to make me feel immature. Therefore, I did not do it. Next, Murph carried a garbage can over his head and placed it next to the swimming pool's fence. Then he climbed to the top of the fence. After he jumped from the top of the fence to the cement landing which was between the fence and the pool, he dusted himself off from a harmless fall to the ground. Then he asked Ray to thrust the can over the fence to him. When it was obvious that Ray couldn't lift it high enough, I helped him push it higher and practically threw it over the fence. It fell on the cement on the other side of the fence with a loud thud. Not sure what Murph planned to do with the garbage can since a plastic-looking material covered the pool for the winter season, I watched intently. I was hoping he wouldn't try to remove the pool's covering and put the garbage can in the pool. That would have made even more racket. What he ended up doing was climbing up the ladder to where the high diving board was during the summer. It was removed during the winter. Once up there, he seemed to be examining the metal structure for a little while. Then he came back down the ladder and struggled to climb back up the ladder while holding the garbage can. Though he looked hysterical doing it, he somehow managed to do it without falling and hurting himself. After he balanced the garbage can on the top rung of the ladder, he scurried down the ladder and quickly climbed the fence again to come back to us on the outside of the pool's fence. As he dusted himself off and tried to catch his breath, he had a great look of self-satisfaction across his face. Then he said, "Neat, huh?" Then he turned to me and said, "I can trust you not to tell, right?" I said,

"Of course, I wouldn't do that." Then he spoke to both Ray and me when he said, "If any of the cool guys ask who did this, say I did. If any little kids or adults ask, play dumb." I asked, "Are you sure? Some older kids might tattle as quickly as little kids." His response was, "I'm sure. Older kids would be afraid that I'd beat them up if I ever found out they told on me." After a pause, he said, "I'd probably never hit anybody unless they hit me first, but other guys don't know that. I know I look mean and frighten some people. Sometimes that's a good thing 'cause the thugs are afraid to mess with me." He wasn't bragging. He was being honest.

The garbage can in the swimming pool diving board's ladder wasn't the last surprise of the night. Next, Murph took out a pack of Marlboro cigarettes and matches from his boot. I tried not to look too surprised but probably failed in the attempt. He gave Ray a cigarette, struck a match, and then lit Ray's cigarette. Then he asked me, "You smoke?" I said, "No, not really." Ray took his cigarette out of his mouth and said, "What do you mean, not really? Either you smoke or you don't." Before I could say another word, Murph ordered Ray to stop by saying, "Let up on him, man!" Murph put a cigarette in his own mouth, grabbed Ray's lit cigarette, and then lit his own off of it. It looked natural to see a tough guy like Murph smoke a cigarette. However, seeing Ray take a long drag on a cigarette looked odd. Ray wasn't acting like the guy I'd known since first grade at all. He pressed the issue by asking me, "Do you want to try it or not?" Murph said, "I said leave him alone!" Then Murph reasoned, "He can have a drag of mine if he wants to try it. Why waste a whole cigarette if he doesn't know if he'll even like it?" Raising his full, dark eyebrows in question, Murph offered me his cigarette by holding it between his thumb and first finger. All I'd ever assumed about smoking was that a person was supposed to be older, an adult, to do it. In addition, I'd heard it stunted people's growth, or maybe coffee was the thing that stunted growth. Maybe it was that both smoking and coffee stunted growth. I wasn't sure and didn't care since I didn't do either up to that point. Even though Murph managed to make me feel comfortable in refusing to try smoking, I contemplated the offer. Since I was the second tallest kid in my class, a negative effect on my growth wasn't an issue. My curiosity as to what smoking was like is what won out.

I reached for the cigarette, slowly put it to my lips, puffed a little, and blew any smoke that got in my mouth right out. Not much got in my mouth. Ray laughed his condescending laugh, and then said, "What a pansy!" Pansy, by the way, was what Ray called guys he often criticized for acting more like a frightened little girl instead of a boy. Then he told Murph what the three of us already knew as he said, "He didn't even inhale." I hated when people talked about me in the third person when I was standing right there. Since I was there, Ray should have spoken directly to me and said that I didn't even inhale. Instead, he awkwardly acted like I wasn't there and said, "He didn't even inhale." It's stupid and condescendingly rude when people do that. Ray was an expert at being condescending.

Anyway, at that, I took a bigger puff of the cigarette, held it in a few seconds longer, and then blew the smoke out slowly. I tried to act like I was even enjoying it. Ray must have been impressed as he quit laughing at me after that. I tried to make my face look like holding the smoke in didn't bother me. But, I wished I had a glass of water to rinse my mouth out. Since that wasn't possible, I wanted to spit. However, I didn't just then.

From a short distance away in the darkness of the playground, I heard a voice shout, "Scott smokes!" I couldn't believe it. In my whole life, this was the first big thing I had done wrong. From the sound of the girl's voice, I knew it was Bonnie. She was one of the older girls who sat next to me in band and she had caught me smoking. It wouldn't have been cool to show my concern in front of Murph and Ray, so I tried to forget about her seeing me puff on the cigarette and continued being grown up with the two guys. Even though Ray was making me feel more accepted since I'd satisfactorily puffed on the cigarette, I still sensed that he would have preferred that I wasn't there. I guess he was the type of person who only liked dealing with one friend at a time. Being sort of a boring kid, he probably didn't like the competition of having to be entertaining in a crowd of three people.

Heading home, Murph and I dropped Ray off first since he lived closest. Then I walked a little further with Murph to the corner where he would turn to go to his house. He asked me where I lived and promised to come over sometime. As I continued walking to my house, my happy thoughts about having found a new friend were replaced by worrisome realities. First, I might have been in trouble for having abandoned Sue and Brett more than an hour ago. Looking at my watch, I saw that I should have probably gotten home earlier, even though Mom and Dad would have probably expected me to stay out a little later on Halloween as long as I wasn't alone. My other concern had to do with Bonnie. If she were to open her big mouth about me smoking, I'd be in big trouble.

When I got home, Mom said, "Hey, mister, I noticed a piece of soap missing from the bathroom sink. Did you and your friend soap windows?" I said, "No, by the time we got to the school, the windows were already soaped enough." She lectured, "At the school? This late? Good way to lose your life, young man! You know the Saints hang around there at night, don't you? I thought you were smarter than that!" She continued, "You stay away from that area except during school hours!" Mothers do dramatize, don't they? Then she said, "Someone got to our windows when I wasn't looking. I don't know how. Get out there and get the soap off the windows for your dad before he gets home from work tomorrow. You'll have to use a razor blade to scrape it off. Be careful not to cut yourself."

That night, before I went to bed, I made sure I talked to Sue, just to make sure she wasn't mad at me for leaving her alone with Brett. As always, everything was okay with us. I went to bed feeling grown up. I got a real kick out of being bad with a bad boy, though I really didn't think Murph was all that bad now that I had met him. Yes, he apparently got kicked out of his last school, hung around with bad kids at our school, pulled pranks, and smoked. But he was nice to me. More than that, he seemed to like me. I hadn't made a new friend in a long time and it felt good to have a new one. I decided that when I would see him at school, I'd discretely nod or wave to him. I'd let him speak first. After all, maybe he had two sides like Ray does. Maybe he wouldn't want his school friends, the bad kids, to know that he'd made a friend of a good kid. Then, since I turned over garbage cans in the schoolyard and took two puffs from Murph's cigarette, I wondered if I was really a good kid anymore.

For a second, it felt good to think that maybe I wasn't a good kid anymore and wouldn't have to live up to that good kid image I'd always had. Being bad on occasion would be so much easier than being good all the time. If a guy is bad at times, people are happy with him when he is good because it's unexpected behavior from him. If a guy is usually good, it's no big deal when he's good because it's his expected behavior. Like tonight, when Ray and Murph smoked, I was disappointed in Ray because he had always been good, or so I thought. But I wasn't disappointed in Murph because I expected him to do even worse things due to his bad reputation. I was happy with him because he lived up to his reputation without doing anything real terrible, like breaking or stealing stuff. These were the things I'd expect a real bad kid to do.

In bed, I pictured Ray standing as he did tonight, thinking he was cool because he knew how to inhale a cigarette. It was strange how I thought so much less of him when I saw him smoke and how he appeared to think so much more of me when I finally took the healthy puff of the cigarette. I always thought Ray and I got along as well as we did because we were so much alike. Now, I was confused. I was beginning to wonder if we were really alike after all. After wondering which Ray was the real one, the one I knew at school for all these years or the one I'd seen tonight, I realized that it didn't matter anyway. Ray would always be one way at school and another way around a kid like Murph who he felt he needed to impress by being bad.

Before falling asleep, I also thought of how disappointed my parents would have been if they'd seen me try a cigarette. A chill ran through my body. If I had had this thought at the school playground tonight, I wouldn't have touched that cigarette. Suddenly debating whether I would be a good or bad kid from now on wasn't necessary. As soon as I thought of my parents being disappointed and of what my parents' reaction would be, I forgot about being bad. If my parents knew I had smoked, I pretty much knew what would have happened. I would have been sent to my room for one night, maybe longer. My recently purchased phonograph and radio would be taken out of my room to make me even more miserable. Mom would threaten not to let me eat meals, but she would eventually bring a plate to my bedroom after the rest of the family had eaten. The hot foods would be kind of cold, though. Then I'd have to come out of my bedroom to do dishes, both washing and drying, all alone. In addition, every time Mom would speak to me, she would talk in a disgusted tone of voice and probably even call me Scott Fred, include my middle name as she sometimes did when she was mad at me, instead of just calling me Scott. At the end of the punishment period, I would get a short but stern talk about why I shouldn't smoke. Of course, Mom would give this lecture instead of Dad because my dad smoked. I was almost positive that I would never smoke again, anyway, since I didn't like it. After thinking about how my parents would react to my being bad, I tried to forget about being bad ever again. Then I finally fell asleep.

The Halloween of 1960 was the day my mind and soul had an appointment to meet the eerie concept of death. After all the worrying I had done about the day, I was too busy to make it to that appointment. It was strange that the day I dreaded so much turned out to be such an interesting day. Rather than Halloween in fifth grade being a day I ignored due to my fears and confusions about Grandpa's death, it turned out to be a day I would remember forever. More than that, it was a day I would remember fondly.

Chapter Ten: Guilty

The next morning, I woke up and stayed in bed since Mom hadn't called me for breakfast yet. As the thoughts of the night before raced through my mind, I was too excited to relax and fall back to sleep. In fact, I didn't even look at my watch, hoping I had lots of time before I'd have to get up. If I only had a few more minutes, I really didn't want to know. I thought about how funny the two extremely different sides of Ray were. At one o'clock yesterday afternoon, he was putting a silly wolf's mask over his face and glasses because his mom told him to do so. Then at seven o'clock in the evening, he was acting tough and smoking a cigarette like a grown up. I softly laughed out loud at his contrasting personalities. My laughing must have stirred Brett because I heard him move around in the bottom bunk. Thankful that he didn't get up, I tried only to laugh silently after that. I didn't want to wake him because I would then have to be cautious about having fun with my thoughts. He wouldn't understand, probably no one would understand, that I liked staying in bed sometimes to replay things from days past that were still in my head. When I had a real good or exciting time, I liked to relive it by thinking it through again. That's what I was still doing when Mom knocked on the door to get us up on this Tuesday morning. She said she was getting us up earlier than usual because she did us the favor of not touching our candy but wanted us to put it away before we left for school.

First, we had some oatmeal with milk and a banana for breakfast. After Sue and Brett left the kitchen, Mom asked me quietly yet firmly, "Did you smoke a cigarette last night?" I wanted to drop to my knees, clasp my hands together tightly and ask the Lord which was worse, lying or smoking. But I needed to cough up an answer now. So almost uncontrollably, the negative response flew out of my mouth, "No!" I sung the long vowel ending of the word so it sounded like the answer people give when they really mean to ask the question: why would you ask such a silly thing? "Oh," Mom shot back a bit louder, "who was then?" After a brief pause, she continued, "When I took clothes out of the hamper this morning, I smelled smoke on the shirt you wore last night." I thought to myself, boy, Mom is smart, too smart to be fooled. But then again, I used to tell myself with intended bad grammar that mama didn't raise no fool! So, staying as calm as I could, I said, "Ray smokes." Of course, that wasn't a lie but an effort to fool my mom. Then I continued, "But don't tell anyone." The implication was that I promised Ray that I wouldn't tell anyone. Mom said, "That really surprises me. I thought that friend of yours had better sense. He doesn't smoke around his mother, does he?" I said, "I don't think so." I didn't mention Murph since I saw no benefit in bringing a new name into the conversation. In fact, the way things were going, the less I could say the better.

However, I didn't really promise Ray that I wouldn't tell anyone that he smokes. He just would have assumed I wouldn't since we were friends. But I didn't think Mom would tell Ray's mom. Why would she? She probably always told Dad everything. As long as it wouldn't go further than that, I wouldn't have to worry about Ray finding out that I had told my mom. What I felt terrible about, naturally, was lying to Mom. As far as I could remember back, this was the first time I had lied to her. I was surprised how quickly and easily the denial came rolling off my tongue and out of my mouth when I said I hadn't smoked. I was either becoming a very good actor or turning into a person who could lie very well. I wouldn't mind being a good actor, but I sure didn't want to become a liar. However, at that moment, I figured that being a believable liar was better than being an admitted smoker.

A kid in our class named Noga lies often. Noga, incidentally is his last name. Nobody, not even teachers, calls him by his first name. Therefore, I don't know what his first name is. Already this year, he told kids about his Dad's big important job in downtown Chicago when his mom had told my mom that his dad was between jobs and needed work. I overheard my mom tell my dad that Noga's mom wanted to know if they were hiring down at Sears where my dad worked a second job, part-time. Another day, he was bragging to Miss McCauley, in front of the whole class, about the new Cadillac his dad had bought. Patty, a girl who lives close to him said, "You know that ain't true, Noga. Your daddy don't drive no Caddy. He's got nothin' but that ol' Chevy station wagon that's a-rustin' away in your driveway. And it ain't moved in over a month." Noga ignored her and created all kinds of details about this imaginary automobile that he must have seen in a magazine or on a television commercial. It was so sad to witness. There was no reason for me to ever talk to Noga. Of anything he could possibly ever have said to me, I would never know if it was true or a product of his wild imagination.

Nevertheless, I wanted to tell Mom the truth. However, other than to clear my conscience, there seemed no need to do so right then. If I had admitted smoking, I would have to pay the consequences immediately. If I were to get caught lying, the consequences wouldn't come until I'd get caught. Also, if I weren't to ever get caught in this lie, I wouldn't have to worry about smoking and getting caught again because I didn't even like having the cigarette in my mouth. Why would I ever do it again? If anybody at school should ever ask me if I smoked, I would honestly say yes. If they were to offer me a cigarette, I would tell them that I don't want one. Both responses would be true. Then they wouldn't think I'm a pansy, as Ray would sometimes call me.

My excuse to get out of the kitchen with Mom was an easy and logical one. I told her that I needed to put my candy away as she had told us to do. Actually, I just threw it in my socks drawer in my bedroom. There was no reason to be particular about putting it anywhere since it wouldn't last long. I'd probably eat it all in a day or two. When I went out to the living room, I saw that my little brother and all his candy from last night were sitting on the living room floor in front of the television. I walked in, gave Brett a smile even though he wasn't looking my way, and I said, "You can't eat all that, Brett. Might as well share it before it rots away." Sitting on the floor with his skinny legs and arms crossed, he was in control of the situation. He was usually in control of situations at our house because he's the youngest. The lucky boy could usually get away with doing most anything. Anyway, Brett was totally ignoring me, which really annoyed me. He was ignoring me even though I was only trying to have a quick and simple conversation with him. That's what he usually did. If I did that to him, he'd run and tell Mom that I wouldn't talk to him. Mom then would tell me to be nice to him or go to my room. There was no way I was going to run and tell on him, though, because I'm sure Mom would have told me to just leave him alone if he didn't want to talk. In this house, according to the adults, Brett was usually right. Or maybe it was just easier to let him have his way than to deal with him.

To say I resented it would be putting it too mildly. What made it worse was that Brett was very smart for a little kid. I think he knew he was in control and therefore played it for all it was worth. And I'm smart enough to know that it's nice when a person in control likes you. Unfortunately, Brett didn't seem to like me at all sometimes. Actually, the only big thing I didn't like about him was that he didn't like me. Other than that, there weren't many reasons for me not to like him. No, I didn't like when he ignored me, or when he ate with his mouth open, or when he would interrupt me when I was talking to someone, or when he wouldn't wash his hands, especially when he had his finger in his mouth or some other hole in his face. Oh, and I hated it when he wet the bed because the whole room would stink until Mom or Dad would come and change his sheets. Come to think of it, I guess there were quite a few things I didn't like about him. Nevertheless, as I said, the worst thing was that he didn't seem to like me. Even thinking about one of Mom's most memorable quotes didn't help me feel much better. Mom would say, "Don't react to people who are mean to you because you never know the real troubles they're having in their lives. It's probably not even you that's making them mean and miserable." While all of that sounded good, at this moment, Brett's only problems were that he was spoiled rotten and had too much chocolate stuffed in his mouth.

Since he just stared at the television and didn't even look my way, I thought about testing him by taking some of the candy that wasn't right in front of him. Of course, if he saw me do it and didn't like my move, he'd either swing at me or yell for Mom. Then I would get nothing. So, I decided to just look for a while. Brett was a picky eater, even when it came to candy. He had all the completely chocolate candy and bubble gum in two piles near his triangularly crossed legs. From my past observations of this character we call Brett, I believed these were the only things, out of all the things he trick-or-treated for last night, which he would eat. In addition, if his tiny stomach didn't feel well before he finished, it would be all the better because then he would get mad and walk away from it all.

Farther away from his legs, he had several piles of different kinds of candy and goodies. One pile was the weird, non-chocolate candies like peppermints, licorice, taffy, and lollipops. Another pile was the stuff that was homemade or not wrapped, such as taffy apples, frosted cupcakes and other bakery goods, and pieces of fruit. They were the things Mom usually had us throw away. Another pile was chocolate bars and candies that weren't completely chocolate, like chocolate Hershey's bars with some kind of nuts in them. He must have visited a few houses that gave out change instead of candy because he had small stacks of pennies, nickels, and dimes on the floor, too. For a little kid, he was so incredibly organized when he did things like this. That's one of the reasons I thought he was very smart for his age. Anyway, in the past, it appeared as though he would only eat totally chocolate candy, nothing else. He ate things like chocolate candy bars, Tootsie Rolls, chocolate Hershey's Kisses, and chocolate Tootsie Roll Pops that were chocolate suckers. He wouldn't eat any other flavors of these scrumptious edibles. I hoped he'd always be this weird about tastes in candy. Then, of course, there would be more for Sue and me. I would eat anything that was there except for licorice, peppermints, taffy, and fruit. Suddenly, without turning his head or moving his eyes from the television set, Brett said, "You can speak now. It's commercial." I said, "Oh, sorry I interrupted your cartoons before. What I was saying was that I can take some of this candy off your hands for you." Still, without even giving me the courtesy of a turned head, let alone eye contact, he commanded, "Throw out the unwrapped pile because Mom says we can't eat it. Then, you may come back and take what you want from the piles left over there. Those are for you and Sue, whoever gets them first. If they're not out of here before you leave for band practice, I'm taking them to school for my friends." While he talked, I looked at his profile and saw gobs of chocolate Hershey bar packed between his teeth. I could never stand to watch him eat because he would talk with his mouth full. Sue and I weren't allowed to do that.

As he had dictated, I scooped up all the unwrapped items and headed to the wastebasket next to the refrigerator in the kitchen. While I was there, I spotted the box of Velveeta cheese and had a nice slice of it. I loved American cheese. Then I hurried back to the living room and divided up the other candies, which Brett said were for Sue and me. Divided quickly and close to evenly, I put half on Sue's bed and the rest in my socks drawer in my room.

When I returned to the living room, still without taking his eyes off the television, he said, "You forgot the M&M's, dummy." For candy, I would even take this name-calling abuse, momentarily, without back-talking him. There would be plenty of time for that after I would devour the candy. He had two piles of opened M&M's. One pile was all of the brown ones and the other pile was all the other colored M&M's. To me, they all tasted about the same. But Brett wanted nothing to do with anything that didn't even look chocolate, I guess. If the M&M's had nuts in them, he didn't even open those packages. Therefore, I divided them up and added the wrapped M&M's to Sue's pile and to my stash in my drawer. Since I had never seen the kid wash his hands, I threw the unwrapped M&M's that he had touched in the garbage to spare Sue and me his germs.

Not getting along with Brett all the time didn't worry me. After all, other than Sue, I didn't know many kids who said they got along with their younger brothers and sisters all the time. So, in this way, I was normal for a change. Of course, Mom and Dad would have been happier if Brett and I could have gotten along better than we did. As it was, if I said yes, he would say no. If he'd say yes, I'd say no. That's how it was. Yet, I knew that I would often get the blame for us not getting along. I would be blamed not only because I was the older one, but also because I apparently had some mystical power, which would get us to cooperate with one another. However, I had no such power. Here's how I saw it. Brett didn't even want or need to be friends with me because he had so many friends in the neighborhood. Many kids in the neighborhood were his age. There was only one kid in our immediate area that was in my grade or my age. I heard one kid about a block-and-a-half away was my age, but he went to a Catholic school down in Joliet so I didn't know him at all. Don't ask me why, but all these little kids in the neighborhood who were Brett's age seemed to like him a lot. So, again, he really didn't need my friendship.

As I put some of the candy in my lunch box, I was reassuring myself that lying about smoking was my best bet with Mom, even though I felt rotten and very sinful about it. But it was getting late. I would have to worry about not going to heaven later. When the idea of getting caught ran through my mind last night, I never thought the threat of getting caught would happen so fast. I thought my only threat would be Bonnie, the wicked girl in band. She couldn't have told anyone yet, even if she wanted to squeal. All I could do is hope and pray that she wouldn't tell everyone her news about me. At that, Sue and I had to walk fast because we were going to be later than late to band. As we left, I told Mom, "See you later." She said, "Not if I see you first." Then she laughed and gave me a little hug. She didn't joke around with me much, but I liked it a lot when she did.

Just before Mr. Mattei stood on the podium to begin band rehearsal that morning, when it gets very quiet just after 8 o'clock, Bonnie, in her strong and confident yet whiny voice, said, "Scott smokes!" I froze. No one reacted, not even Mr. Mattei. He ignored her outburst, stepped on the podium, raised his arms for us to put our instruments in playing position, and we started practicing our national anthem for an upcoming assembly. I realized that Bonnie resented the fact that I, only a fifth-grade student, sat one chair ahead of her. However, I didn't know that her jealousy had made her hate me enough to do something that mean to me. Maybe everyone assumed she made it up to hurt me. At least, I'd hoped that's what they'd think. If she'd said I tried two puffs of a cigarette last night, which was the truth, it wouldn't have bothered me as much. She made it look like I was a nicotine addict. My only consolation was that everyone knew I'd be too shy to correct her or to argue with her. And these band kids also knew that she was loud most of the time to get attention. She was a girl that very few bold kids would even verbally tangle with, let alone someone shy like me. Her abrasive manners made her appear to be more like a bad boy than like a young lady. She didn't dress or look like a tomboy, but she acted like one. She was a bully. When she sat one chair ahead of me instead of behind me last year, she got mad about something and hit me in my arm. I felt so bad that she hit me and appeared to hate me for no good reason that tears started falling from my eyes. I didn't make any crying sounds, but I couldn't stop the sad tears from falling. Mr. Mattei looked at me and softly said, "Never cry in front of a girl. Go wash your face off." I went to the washroom way down at the other end of the gymnasium and did as he said to do. When I got back, Bonnie said, "I didn't hit you that hard." I ignored her. Even if it hadn't been for her harsh style, I had always kept my mouth shut around these older kids in the front row. By not defending myself in this smoking situation, I was doing what people would have expected of me. I could only hope that my silence was not considered an admission of guilt.

I just stared at the music sitting on the music stand in front of me, hoping to see Mr. Mattei's hand-motioned instructions from the corner of my eye. I was afraid to make eye contact with anyone. Most of all, I didn't want to meet eyes with Mr. Mattei. I wouldn't want him to be ashamed of me since my only dealings with him had been very positive. And maybe that's why Bonnie tried to embarrass me. Due to my musical abilities, I guess, I appeared to be one of Mr. Mattei's favorite students. Then again, maybe Mr. Mattei wouldn't care much if he really did think I smoked. After all, he was a smoker, himself. He was a cigar smoker.

As we continued playing song after song, I felt anger replacing the embarrassment about what Bonnie had done. But my shyness didn't allow me to do anything more than swallow every bit of anger I had within me. In that way, I guess shyness was a good thing. If I'd displayed anger, it wouldn't have done me any good. In fact, it probably would have made me look guilty as charged by Bonnie.

Either my sister didn't hear Bonnie's comment about me smoking or she didn't care to comment on it later because she never even mentioned it at home. I was incredibly thankful for that, naturally. Apparently, the smoking issue had burned out. In fact, Sue was just as nice as ever even though I had left her stuck with Brett the night before. But being older and the one who wanted to have a third kid in the family, she should have been the one who'd have to take care of the youngest when Mom and Dad weren't around.

Don't get me wrong. I liked having a little brother most of the time. It's just that when Mom and Dad announced years ago that we would be having a brother or sister joining us, I only took the news with interest. My sister, however, got all excited and talked non-stop about it until Mom finally brought Brett home from the hospital. Though I didn't really mind having the new baby in the family, I was quite content with the family of four we'd had before he came along. When the day of my brother's birth neared, I remember how Sue kept saying that she wanted the baby to be a girl. Following her lead, I naturally acted as if I wanted the new baby to be a boy. Honestly, I didn't care what Mom had. When Brett was finally born, I felt sorry for Sue. As much as she talked about wanting a baby girl to be the new member of the family, I think she may have really meant it. I shouldn't have hoped for a boy or a girl since I really didn't care which one Mom had. I wouldn't want to think that Sue missed out on having a little sister simply because my hoping power was stronger than hers. But Sue obviously never minded that she got another brother instead of a sister. She couldn't have loved Brett more.

One thing I didn't want, however, was for Mom to have twins. The older and bigger my sister and I got, the smaller that '56 Chevy car in the driveway seemed to become. It was a stylish blue and white Bel Air. Although Mom would hold the new baby in the front seat for a while, I figured it wouldn't be long before she'd get tired of holding the baby and start putting him in the back seat between Sue and me. That would make it even more crowded in the back seat. If Mom had had twins, I'd have to be forceful in letting my parents know that we'd have to get a station wagon so I could be by myself way in the back of the car behind the second seat most of the time. I didn't want to have to do that. Therefore, I was delighted when Mom brought only one baby home from the hospital. Though his dirty diapers, loud crying, louder screaming, and throwing up were the grossest things I had ever seen, it wasn't as bad as when he actually started talking.

Anyway, my two fears of the evening proved to be unfounded. No one in the family said anything about my not trick-or-treating with my brother and sister very long or about me smoking last night. Therefore, I was quite worry-free and relaxed when Dad and I took a trip to the gas station and the neighborhood market. This was a time when gas cost much less and the workers at the station did much more. Even though the gas station attendant came out to the car and put the gas in the tank for customers, my dad got out of the car and talked to the man. Either he was a friend of my dad's or my dad just knew him well from getting gas at the same station often. Besides putting gas in the tank, this man washed the windshield and raised the car's hood to check the oil. He also collected the money for the gas so customers wouldn't have to enter the gas station's building. It was like going to a drive-in or drive-through business where customers didn't have to get out of their vehicles if they didn't want to get out. The cost of gas in 1960 was 28 cents a gallon, which was up a whole nickel since the year I was born in 1950. Though I'm not positive, I think a quart of oil for my dad's car cost the same as a gallon of gas. It wasn't long after that time that things started changing as prices started to rise a little and gas station workers were doing much less work for the customers. Anyway, after getting home from gassing up the car and buying milk, Mom said a boy named Michael stopped by to see me. I asked, "Michael?" She said, "Yes, a polite and very nice-looking young man named Michael Murphy. He said everyone calls him Murph." I was so glad that he'd stopped by, but I was even gladder that I missed him tonight since I had lots of homework to do and sleep to catch up on. Last night, the excitement of Halloween didn't allow me to get enough sleep. It would have taken quite a bit of energy to be alert and cordial to a new friend. I would be able to do this better after getting some good sleep.

Every time Murph stopped by for the next week or so, I was always out of the house. Either I was at basketball practice, the church's Youth Group, or my clarinet lesson when he stopped by. When I finally saw him on the playground that Friday, we approached one another. When he saw me, he had that big smile that he had the night Ray took me to his house. With that greeting, I knew he wouldn't mind being friends at school as well as away from school. When I told him that my mom said he stopped by the house a couple of times, he asked, "Hey, are you ever home?" I told him that I was only home on Tuesday and Friday nights most weeks. He told me that he thought it was great that I had so much to do.

Suddenly, this king of cool appeared to be the king of loneliness when he said, "It must be nice to have something to do after dinner. Other than watching television or playing pool in the basement by myself, I'm always looking for some place to go or something to do." He said it with a little laugh in his voice, but I could tell he meant it. I asked, "Don't you ever do anything with your brothers or sisters?" He said, "I don't have any brothers or sisters. It's just me and my mom and dad."

I suggested that he check with the school's basketball coach, Mr. Piazza, to see if he could still go out for basketball this season. He said, "Nah, Scott. I'm not much of an athlete at all. I don't even know the rules of the game." Surprised with his admission, I gave some honesty right back by saying, "Well, I'm bad at sports, too, but

I go out. Why don't you go out? We might have some fun before the coach starts cutting players from the list. That's when my season is sure to end." He said, "I don't think so, but I'll think about it." I really hoped he would so that I could be with someone at practice who wasn't very athletic like me. Having Murph there would give me time to get to know him better, too. Then the bell rang and we had to line up with our classes to go back inside our classrooms.

Chapter Eleven: John F. Kennedy

Living in the year 1960 was exciting for a kid. It was probably quite exciting for adults, too. I got most of the news about the world by listening to my parents. They talked about the possibility of another World War since the United States and Russia weren't getting along. Last school year, United States President Dwight D. Eisenhower and Russian leader Nikita Krushchev were talking about making peace with one another. Then, during May of last school year, the Russians shot down an American spy plane. The embarrassing incident for the United States ended talks of peace, naturally.

The United States wasn't getting along with Cuba either since Fidel Castro was another one of President Eisenhower's enemies. Just the year prior to this, in 1959, Castro had become the prime minister of the Republic of Cuba. Having all these problems, it may have been fate that President Eisenhower couldn't be president for more than two terms since the 22nd Amendment was ratified regarding presidential term limits in 1951. One term is four years, so he was president for eight years. Talk was that Eisenhower was popular enough to have won a third term as president if the 22nd Amendment had not limited him to two. Then it was rumored that he didn't want the job any longer anyway. Consequently, due to the Amendment to the Constitution, which passed during President Harry S Truman's term, Eisenhower's time was up whether he wanted the job or not. One odd thing I remember about President Harry S Truman was that his middle initial wasn't supposed to have a period after it. To make this more confusing, there were times Truman, himself, actually used a period after his middle initial. As the story goes in history books, the S after Truman's first name wasn't actually an abbreviation for a definite middle name. It stood for a couple of people, Anderson Shipp Truman and Solomon Young. With or without the written period after the S after his first name, he was the president just before Eisenhower. It seemed odd that I liked hearing about current events so much when I really didn't like history class at all in school. After all, current events stories that my parents talked about so often were history in the making.

The men who were running against each other to become Eisenhower's replacement as president were Vice President Richard M. Nixon and Senator John F. Kennedy. Even though Nixon held a higher office, Kennedy seemed to be the one who most people were talking about as the election approached. That fall, I almost shook hands with Senator Kennedy. I'd truly like to say I did shake his hand, but honestly, I didn't quite do it. Kennedy was in a motorcade that drove through Joliet. His arrival was scheduled for six o'clock on the mild, clear evening of October 24, 1959. Dad took us in the family car a couple of miles from our house to a new outdoor strip mall, Hillcrest, which would be officially opening a few weeks later with Illinois Governor William Stratton in attendance at an official ribbon cutting ceremony. We stood along the motorcade route near the north end of the strip mall where a huge store that hadn't officially opened just yet, called the Boston Store, was located. There, along the motorcade at Larkin and Plainfield Roads, traffic was the worst I had ever seen it in the area. In the massive crowd, it seemed like we had to wait forever for Kennedy's late arrival, but I think it was actually only about ninety minutes. That is when we saw the first cars in the motorcade, which were escorting Kennedy into the city. As each car in the line of cars passed, the more excited I became. I pushed and crept my way to the front of the crowd to get the best look possible before Kennedy's car would go by.

First, I saw a few cars carrying people who looked important, but I didn't recognize any of them. They acted famous as they nonchalantly waved their arms and hands as if they were royalty, some movie star, a famous singer, or somebody else who was famous. They were probably Democratic politicians who were running for an office somewhere in Illinois in the same election cycle. Finally, the police-escorted car crawled up that I assumed was carrying Kennedy as the crowd went wild. Then I could see that it was Kennedy's vehicle. There was a chauffeur in a black suit driving the long, black convertible with its top opened. Also, there were at least two men walking on each side of the car who watched the crowd intently. These men who were dressed in black suits and talking into walkie-talkies must have been Kennedy's bodyguards. Just steps away from me, John F. Kennedy sat on top of the back seat of the opened car while leaning to his right to reach out and shake people's hands. Even though the bodyguards were trying to keep everyone back on the sidewalk, hardly anyone was obeying their hand and arm motions. Just before Kennedy got up to me, the crowd pressed forward even harder than before. As the car crawled by very, very slowly, Kennedy stopped shaking hands with the people on the right side of the car where I was standing. Probably due to the crowd's aggressiveness, he brought his hand back into the vehicle and casually pushed his hair up off his forehead with his right hand and continued to smile. At that very moment, he looked me right in the eye while still holding that incredible smile that I had seen so often on television and in the newspapers. I just knew that I would always remember that very moment in time because I knew there was very little chance I would ever be that close to a famous presidential candidate again in my entire life. I also couldn't help thinking how very tired he looked. Of all the times I'd seen him on television, I'd never seen him look this exhausted. Then, as one of the bodyguards knocked me out of his way with great force, I eased back to the sidewalk with everyone else. Being behind Kennedy by then, I could see him turn to his left, lean over, and begin shaking hands on the other side of his vehicle. I kept staring until the crowd blocked my view. If the crowd hadn't become so intense on my side of his car and if Kennedy wouldn't have pushed the hair over his forehead up to the top of his head at just the moment he did, I know I would have gotten to shake his hand. As it was, though, I only brushed his vehicle just before his bodyguard bumped me hard. I was so mad at that bodyguard for interfering with my important moment. Though I was very disappointed that I didn't shake his hand, and though I was somewhat tempted to exaggerate the truth, I never exaggerated about it. I would always have to admit that I was that close to John F. Kennedy and, by my standards, botched it somehow. I should have yelled to him, "Please shake my hand!" or "Good luck, Mr. Kennedy!" But I didn't. I never told anyone how close I came to shaking his hand. Why would they care about my Kennedy incident since I didn't shake his hand?

That night, as the family drove back home from the Joliet gathering, I sat still on the left side of the back seat, behind Dad. That's where I usually sat when all of us were in the car. I was thinking how stupid I was for being that close to John F. Kennedy and not being able to think of one thing to say to him. Instead of wishing him success in his bid for the presidency, I just made him feel as uncomfortable as everybody else did. I fought the crowd to gawk at him. It was silly for everyone to act like that. Why couldn't we all have been more civilized by standing on the sidewalk and simply applauding his arrival?

After I said my prayers and checked under the bed again to make sure no one was there, I stayed awake thinking how strange it was that I realized I experienced something I'd never forget. When people have an unforgettable moment, they usually don't realize it until a long time later. It seemed so very strange to me. It was almost as strange as looking under the bed every night. I also thought about the possibility of finally accepting the fact that I now lived in a city called Crest Hill instead of Joliet. My family didn't move, but the borderline of Joliet moved. Earlier in the year, the northern portion of Joliet where I lived broke away from the city of Joliet and became the city of Crest Hill. I didn't like it at all. I was born in Joliet. When I was two-years-old and we moved to the north, we still lived in Joliet. I had lived in Joliet my whole life. Now, I was supposed to say I'm from a place called Crest Hill? Other than getting older, I never liked change very much, and this was a big change. Beyond change, I didn't care for the name because it was hard for me to keep it straight. I would catch myself calling it Hillcrest instead of Crest Hill because that was the name of the strip mall that was opening at Larkin and Plainfield Roads where John F. Kennedy visited. However, I finally reasoned that if the place was good enough for Kennedy to visit, it should be good enough to be my hometown. Though it didn't happen overnight, to say the least, I accepted it in time. Like it or not, I lived in the small city of Crest Hill, which many people had probably never heard of, instead of the big, well-known city of Joliet.

In other current news, the Russians and the United States were continuing to send animals up into space. Actually, Russia started sending dogs into space several years before and was still doing it in 1960. We Americans were sending all kinds of animals, too, including monkeys, dogs, and mice. Actually, fruit flies led the way to the experimentation of sending animals into space as it occurred three years before I was even born, back in 1947. The fruit flies returned alive, but some of the animals that went into space afterward died during the experimental travels. These were big headlines, but I really thought it was pretty stupid to make such a big deal about these stories. I couldn't imagine the two governments spending so much money on something like space travel, unless they were planning to send people way out there into space someday, too. Maybe they assumed that if it worked for animals, it would soon work for humans, too. Then I thought that none of this added up. Why would anyone possibly want to risk his life by going that far away from home, regardless of how much money the job would pay? I sure wouldn't want to go. As it turned out, though, regardless of my initial opinion on the popular topic of the day, Russia and the United States both started sending people into outer space the very next year in 1961.

In 1960, it seemed that Russia was always a step ahead of the United States in space travel. Besides being first with the satellite, they were first to put a human being in space. In terms of national security, one concern for the United States was that Russia allegedly could have reach the United States in 30 minutes through space travel while it would take much longer for the United States to get to Russia with its less sophisticated air travel. The topic was not only very big on the news, but it was a huge political topic, too. In May of 1961, after John F. Kennedy had become President of the United States, he said, "I believe this nation should commit itself to achieving the goal, before this decade is out, of landing a man on the moon and returning him safely to Earth." That happened at 9:56 in the evening on July 20, 1969, when astronaut Neil Armstrong was 240,000 miles away from Earth and set foot on the moon. Sadly, Kennedy was assassinated on November 22, 1963, and he never saw the historic space event happen.

Anyway, it took Armstrong's Apollo 11 spacecraft 76 hours to get to the moon. I was with my family in front of the television set watching as Armstrong stepped on the moon and said, "That's one small step for man, one giant leap for mankind." Some acoustic researchers claim that he actually said, "That's one small step for a man, one giant leap for mankind." Regardless, the United States was the first country on Earth to put a human being on the moon.

Though I wasn't much of a sports fan in fifth grade, I remember the boys at boxing class talking about Cassius Clay. He was an 18-year-old who won an Olympic gold medal for his boxing abilities. Due to the attention he was receiving from the guys and coaches in boxing class, I started watching him on television when I had a chance. He was incredibly good at it. Dad told me how hard a person has to train for sporting successes like Clay had as a boxer. He said that Clay had already fought about a hundred matches and had knocked out about half of his opponents. I had already decided that I didn't want boxing success bad enough to go through all the hours of training every day. Unlike music, where I had more fun creating my own than playing others' songs, I didn't want to be the creative one in a boxing ring. Instead of striving to be a success like Clay, I'd rather be entertained by watching him. He put on a great show when he fought.

Jumping on the trampoline was also a big topic. Even though our school didn't have one, I wished they did. It looked like so much fun. I read that they had been around for years and were just now becoming more popular for entertaining people as people would enjoy jumping on them. People would climb up on a metal circular bar where a material was tightly pulled by rope to the metal edge. Then people would walk or crawl out to the middle of the taut yet elastic material and start jumping up and down. People who were coordinated would jump high and do various somersaults on it while bouncing up into the air. It looked like so much fun. It reminded me of flying through the air from the high diving board into the water at the swimming pool. This wouldn't be as much fun as the high dive, though, because there wouldn't be any swimming or water involved. But, for a winter activity when the outdoor pool in our neighborhood was closed, this would have been great if I had one to jump on. Even though I couldn't use one, it was fun to watch television shows in which others were jumping on them.

In entertainment, the big names in 1960 that I remember were related to television and music. Little Joe and Hoss Cartwright were two brothers that I liked on *Bonanza* and Dennis was the kid on *Dennis the Menace*. Then there were the various characters like Fred, Wilma, Barney, and Pebbles who were very famous on *The Flinstones*. The characters on *The Flinstones* were household names even though they were cartoon characters instead of real people. Since Dad liked cartoons as much as most any kid, we kids didn't have to plead to get to watch this show.

In music, Elvis Presley was still the rage. All of his records continued to do well with the public. It was a year when there were many silly records out, too. The only silly song I liked was *Itsy Bitsy Teenie Weenie Yellow Polka-Dot Bikini*, and I only liked that one because it reminded me of going swimming. I felt that most silly songs were abusing music. Even though I wasn't nearly as into the words in songs as the music, I thought the notes should have been used for something more beneficial. However, from the looks of the WLS Silver Dollar Survey, novelty songs were quite popular. People must have bought many of them and requested them to be played on the radio a lot, too. Brenda Lee, the prettiest singer I'd seen on television, was also very popular. Every song she recorded that was played on the radio station was a top ten record, I think, and sometimes her records went all the way to number one. Around this time, she had a pretty song called *I'm Sorry* that sounded so good to me. The words were sad but the melody was great. I was always interested in the music and not so much the words in songs. Anyway,

I'm Sorry was another song I would eventually keep alive in my memory by playing it on my clarinet and writing down every note. Brenda had a great singing voice, which was so different from the other females' voices on the radio. Sometimes, in my thoughts, I'd pretend that I was older and married to her. It sounds corny, I know. After all, I was only ten years old and she was fifteen. But if I could end up with a lady that pretty, that talented, and that rich and famous, my adult life would be terrific.

Another reason 1960 was an interesting time to be a kid was that a new decade had finally arrived. A new third digit in the year part of the date was being written. It was something other than the 1950s. I could see my age coincide with the year's number, too. Being born in 1950, that was my zero year. In 1951, I was one. In 1952, I was two, and so on. As the fourth digit of the year would change, it would agree with my age after my birthday arrived that year. This year, in 1960, I had finally turned ten years old. It would always be easy to remember the year I was born as well as my age since I'd made this connection between the year of my birth and my age. By 1960, I was feeling much older than I'd felt throughout the 1950s. After all, a decade is a long time, and I'd lived longer than a decade so far, almost eleven years.

I always wished my teachers would have done more with current news at school, especially since I was already interested through my parents' conversations. However, at our school, they must have thought kids wouldn't be interested in these things. Or, maybe the teachers didn't think it was important or educational. I don't know. In fact, the only news-related lesson I remember doing from the time fifth grade started in September until this time in fifth grade was what Miss McCauley and most of our school was doing just before the presidential election of 1960. During the week preceding the November 8th election, Miss McCauley made the first assignment all year that didn't involve us reading pages and writing answers to questions from our textbooks. I wondered how she would grade the current events assignment since it wouldn't be something like twenty questions where there would be five points off from a perfect score of 100 for each one wrong. Anyway, the assignment was to make two signs that were to be the size of a small bumper sticker on a car. These signs would promote the person each student in the class supported in the upcoming election. Eventually the signs would be displayed on the right and left sides of each student's desk. Miss McCauley told us to make a larger sign, too, which we would carry next Monday, the day before the election, in an all-school assembly. Everyone in my class was so excited about the assignment and the upcoming assembly that we forgot to behave ourselves in front of Miss McCauley. For the first time all year, everyone in the class started talking to each other without permission, not even thinking about whether Miss McCauley would get upset or not. For a couple of minutes, she must have not cared because she let us talk excitedly without saying anything. Finally, she must have gotten tired of the noise because she yelled in her deep, gruff tone, "All right, all right! Everyone get quiet and get back to work. You'll have to do your signs at home or during recess because I don't want to lose more book time." In addition, as she often did, she reminded us of our absence of family ties by saying, "If you work on your signs here, clear up after yourselves when you're done. I'm not your mother!" At that, we continued our history assignment, which was to read silently and answer the many questions in the margins of the pages we were reading. I never knew why, but we had to write out the questions and then answer the questions in complete sentences. It involved work, work, and more work, which took time, time, and more time.

The weekend before the election, I started working on the political signs for school. As I was spacing out the letters K-E-N-N-E-D-Y on my sign, Mom walked by the kitchen table, stopped, turned around, and gasped, "What are you doing, Scott?" "My homework," I said. "I could have guessed it was for school, but why are you making a poster for JFK?" she asked in a disgusted tone as she pointed to the name I was penciling on my sign. "Well," I said, "I want Sen. Kennedy to win." Mom gave me her long, cold, you-can't-be-serious look, and I knew a lecture was about to begin. First, before she started, I tried to explain my reasoning by saying, "Mom, if Nixon had come to town and I would've seen him in person, maybe I'd like him better. But, from what I see of him on television, I just don't like the guy." I tried to make my dislike for the man sound like my thoughts, but it was really what I had heard somebody say on the television about him.

"You don't like the guy? And exactly what do you claim to know about him?" Mom screeched. "Well, let me tell you, young man," she continued, "Kennedy is for the Negroes and the poor people." I bravely countered with, "Is there anything wrong with wanting to help them?" She turned red in the face as she screeched louder, "Is there anything wrong with it?" She took several deep breaths before saying, "Ever since FDR, all the Democrats who followed him have turned their backs on the hard-working people in this country. All those Democrats try to do is get the votes of the people who want handouts. If Kennedy wins, hard-working people like your father will have less of a chance in this country. We need another Ike Eisenhower. Since he can't have the job anymore, we'll just have to settle for the next best man, Vice President Nixon. He's got to win!"

I didn't argue with Mom because she had to have known more than I did about this topic. But I did know that in school it was mentioned that Roosevelt could have done even more to help minorities. Yes, programs came into being that helped minorities under his presidency, but some Americans still had been blocked in many ways by some government actions that weren't taken during the Roosevelt years. Disturbing to me, this was the first time I'd ever heard my mom mention the difference between other people and us. She had never referred to the rich or the poor, the Negroes or the whites, or any other separations of people. These separations made me very uncomfortable. I didn't like that the separations existed and that Mom was pointing them out to me. Whether people were the same or not, I wanted to believe all people were the same. I didn't want to have to feel sorry for people who were poorer than we were, and I didn't want to be envious of people richer than us. I'd already done a good job of ignoring it in my friendships with Chuck, who was poorer than us, and Murph, who appeared to be wealthier than my family. And I didn't want to think I should ever dislike someone I didn't know just because he didn't look like me. Besides, the few Negroes who I knew of were very successful people and I liked them. Cassius Clay was someone everyone appeared to like and respect. The men who sang the very popular song on the radio that I liked so much, The Drifters, had the best male singing voices on the radio, so I thought. And Rochester was great on *The Jack Benny Program*. The show would have been missing a lot if he wasn't on it. None of them looked anything like me, but I liked them all and had respect and admiration for each of them. Each one's accomplishments deserved my respect. How could I ever not appreciate them just because they looked different from me? Any other way of thinking wouldn't be right.

I refused to dislike Kennedy for wanting to help poor people like Chuck and for being supportive of people like Cassius Clay, Rochester, and The Drifters. And after looking Kennedy right in the eye and almost shaking his hand, I'd seen him close enough to feel that he was just like us. I didn't understand how he couldn't be good to people like my dad. Yet, as Mom continued to preach the evils of the Democrats, Kennedy in particular, I was thinking about the history book pages I had read regarding the social classes. I was saddened to find that the same separations of differing people exist. One of the reasons I was glad I was living in these times instead of the olden days was because of the separations of people which past generations were expected to honor. Disliking someone for being different, like people did in the history books, seemed so wrong. Beyond not comprehending how I could not like someone just because he wasn't just like me, I sure didn't want anyone else to dislike me just because I wasn't like him.

After Mom left the kitchen, I sat there thinking about everything she had said. The more I thought about it, the more I couldn't accept it. For the first time, so it seemed, I strongly disagreed with her. However, at that moment, I felt a much stronger need to keep peace in the house. Therefore, I reluctantly started the assignment over again. Since I couldn't even vote, I consoled myself by thinking that it didn't matter which signs I would make. If I could have voted, I guess I'd avoid trouble by voting for Kennedy and then never talk about it at home. But since making this poster wouldn't sway the election in either candidate's favor, it really didn't matter how I completed the homework assignment. At least, that's what I told myself.

Besides keeping peace with Mom, one other thing was better about changing my plans from doing Kennedy signs to doing a Nixon signs. Nixon's name had fewer letters, which meant I would finish the assignment faster. When Sue saw me finishing my two signs and poster, she said, "Oh, I was supposed to do that for my class, too. Why don't you just give me one of yours? After I explained that Miss McCauley told my class to make two small ones for each side of our desks as well as a big one for the all-school assembly tomorrow, she started making her own. As my sister quickly lettered the words 'Vote for Nixon,' I asked, "Who do you really want to win, Sue-Sue?" She snapped, "Well, Nixon better win, Scott, or this country will be in big trouble!" I didn't say another word. My mom's impact on her opinion of Kennedy had obviously taken hold. I went to my bedroom to get my clarinet. In the basement, I worked on writing a new song and then figured out how to play some of the songs I had liked on the radio recently. I don't know why, but it seemed as though I could always forget everything that was bothering me when I was playing the clarinet.

After this day's events, I had an increased interest in the presidential election of 1960. I really wanted John F. Kennedy to win. Though I wasn't looking forward to Mom's reaction if he were to win, in time, I figured that Mom would realize what I'd already sensed about Kennedy. Hopefully, she would see that he would be good for everybody, not just for people who weren't like us. And if Mom was right and Kennedy did give extra help to the downtrodden in the United States, it seemed like that would make life better for everyone living in the country. No, I didn't want anyone to get free handouts if they were lazy, as Mom thought would happen. But I wanted everyone to have the chance to work and make money to raise a family like Dad had always done for our family. I hoped Kennedy would do this. Of course, if Nixon would become the next president, I hoped that he could make things better, too. I didn't have much hope of this happening with Nixon as the leader, though. If he could make things better, why didn't he do something while he was the vice president? After all, he was the number two man for the past eight years.

Chapter Twelve: Politics and Prejudices

The day before the election, I entered class a little late because band rehearsal ran overtime. The band was busy practicing hard for tomorrow's all-school political assembly. When I entered the classroom, everyone was busy putting their bumper sticker-type signs on their desks' sides. I decided to tackle the hardest side of my desk first, the inside which faced the "B" row. This side was tougher because I was big and the aisle was narrow. I always did the toughest part of a job first. I reached in my desk and took out my Scotch tape. Then, I found my signs, which I had folded neatly and put in my music folder. I put them upside down on my desk and looped pieces of tape all over the backs of them. I squeezed between the row of desks and the people in the aisle, and I carefully centered one of my signs on the side of my desk. With the palm of my left hand, I pressed firmly on the sign to make sure it would stay. I was also careful not to slide the palm of my hand from side to side or up and down because that might smear the red and blue pencil markings I'd made on the white paper. I thought a political poster should be red, white, and blue like our American flag.

Shortly after I'd put the first sign on my desk, I noticed people looking my way. The noise level of the class rose quickly. Within the louder talking, I heard some snickering. As I saw the crowd from the corner of my eye, I dared to look around and noticed that I was getting looks and snickers that kids get when they come back from the washroom and forget to pull up their zippers. After doing a subtle zipper-check, I tried ignoring the invisible spotlight, which I obviously had beaming down on me. As I finished taping the other sign on the other side of my desk, it seemed as though practically everyone was looking at my desk and me. I took a quick look to make sure I hadn't hung my Nixon sign upside down. Having a big N at each end of his name, I could have carelessly made such a mistake. When I saw that the sign was right side up, I checked for spelling errors. As I assumed, there were none. As shy as I was, this type of attention was really hard on me, especially when I didn't know why I was receiving it.

Suddenly, I felt my face flush as I broke out in a terrible sweat. A horrible thought occurred to me. Could it be that I got all of this attention for being the only Nixon supporter in the entire room? In a panic, I started eyeballing all the other signs that I could see from where I was standing. When I saw nothing but 'Kennedy for President' and 'Vote for Kennedy' signs on desks, I started stretching my neck to see more signs at a further distance from my desk. Though I didn't want to believe it, every other desk that had signs displayed were signs in support of John F. Kennedy. My eyes searched for Ray. Though it didn't surprise me, I was very disappointed to find him sneering at me. Then I looked for Chuck. He wasn't laughing because he was too busy making his signs. He rarely did his homework at home and this assignment was no exception. If he didn't finish his work at school, it didn't get done. He was smart, but getting him to do schoolwork outside of school was nearly impossible. And he was obviously smart enough to add one more Kennedy sign to the room full of Kennedy signs rather than to join me, the lone stranger with Nixon signs. When all signs were posted, there were twenty-nine desks plastered with the name Kennedy. One had the name Nixon, and of course, that desk was mine.

After a while, Miss McCauley told everyone to sit. The many assignments to be done by morning recess were made, and everyone got quiet and began to do the work. For some time thereafter, I got an occasional look of pity, sometimes followed by a smirk. Those casting pity would first make sure I'd seen them. Then they would look down at my Nixon sign. Finally, they would look back at my face, look me right in my eyes, and shake their heads slowly from left to right, left to right, left to right, as if to say what a pitiful loser I was for wanting Nixon to win. Chuck and Ray were both having a lot of fun over my misery. Ray stared at me until I finally looked back. Then he mimicked a hearty laugh by putting his hands over his mouth and rocking back and forth in his seat as if to have a big belly laugh. Chuck wasn't that overly dramatic, but he had little sympathy for my apparent unwise decision to promote Nixon either. He was getting a chuckle out of all this. Finally, the silence was broken when Miss McCauley barked, "Knock it off over there!" No one knew exactly who she was talking to, but she was probably yelling at everybody who was having a good time at my expense.

By recess, it appeared that everyone had forgotten about my Nixon sign, or so I had hoped. Even so, I thought about staying in the room during recess and taking my signs off my desk. But that would just have drawn more attention to my desk and me. The last thing I wanted for the rest of the day was more attention than I'd received when I'd hung up those Nixon signs. So to be sure that I wouldn't be teased during recess, I slithered over by the teachers' parked cars just south of the playground, an area that I would assume was restricted. I sat there in hopes that the fifteen minutes would end without me being caught.

If I were to get caught, though, I had my somewhat true excuse ready. I would say that I felt like throwing up and wouldn't want anyone to have to see me do it. If they asked why I was by the cars instead of in the washroom, I'd say that the fresh air always seemed to make me feel better. When a person tells someone that he feels like throwing up, the other person usually just leaves him alone. So I kept that excuse on the tip of my tongue in case I were to need it. And it really wasn't much of a fib. When I don't feel well like I felt on that day, I usually can make myself feel like throwing up. Yet, I rarely have done it. It was a perfect day for feeling like throwing up, though, since it was Monday, and I usually don't feel very well on Mondays because I'd rather it still be the weekend. So, I reasoned in my mind, I really wouldn't be telling much of a lie if I were to get caught and say that I felt lousy enough to hurl.

After sitting on the gravel for a minute or so, I heard the crunch of gravel coming from a short distance away. I quickly looked under the car next to me and was relieved that I wasn't staring at a pair of big shoes with a teacher's feet in them. Instead, I saw a little face staring at me. Surprised that I wasn't alone, I asked in a startled voice, "What are you doing here?" The little face responded, "The question is: what are you doing here?" Naturally, I said, "I asked you first!" The kid said, "I'm always here. You're the new one here." Being confused, I asked, "You're always here?" He said, "Yup! I'm here every day we have recess outside." Making lots of crumpled gravel noise, the kid crawled under the car and anxiously asked, "So, why did you come here?" Before I could say a word, he continued, "I hate my class! That's why I'm here all the time. Do you hate yours, too?" I said, "Today, I hate mine, too." Then it hit me and I said, "I've seen you before. I've seen you in the principal's office sometimes." "You sent to the office too?" he asked. I said, "No, but I look in the doorway to see who's in there when I've walked by." He offered, "I'm there quite a bit. My teacher can't handle me and puts me in the office when she thinks I'm having a bad day." So I changed the topic by telling him that my class is making fun of me because I brought a Nixon sign to school to put on my desk. The kid, obviously not very up-to-date on current events, asked me, "What's a Nixon sign?" Delighted that he didn't know, and more delighted that he didn't start making fun of me for making the sign, I said, "It's a sign which tells people to vote for Nixon in tomorrow's election." He looked confused and asked me why I would be telling people who to vote for at an elementary school when kids are too young to vote and when the teachers wouldn't care who I thought they should vote for since they had minds of their own. Even though this kid didn't follow current events, he was logical. To change the topic again, I told him my name and he said, "I'm Tim, and I'm in fifth grade. Until this year, I lived with my mom and went to a Chicago school. Now I live with my dad and come here." By the time the bell rang to return to class, I knew quite a bit about him. He seemed to like talking a lot. I guess he was lonely because he not only spent recesses alone but also spent quite a bit of time sitting in the office where there were no kids.

As we started walking up to the other kids, I told him this was the dangerous part because we could be caught coming from the parking lot. He said, "Don't worry about it. The teachers are usually the first ones to head for the door when the bell rings. They don't look around. They just keep talking to each other and drinking their coffee until most of the kids get back in the building. Then they start looking around to see if everybody got back inside before they shut the door." He really had this hide-and-seek routine figured out. Not knowing who Nixon was, I thought he wasn't very school-smart. However, he appeared to be very playground-smart. As we kept walking to the school, I learned that he lived on the far end of town, like Chuck. He also said he knew where I lived because he had seen me in my yard some days when he was walking home from school. I thought that all kids who lived as far away from school as he did would take the bus. Even Chuck, as poor as his mom appeared to be, took the bus. Therefore, I figured that Tim's dad had less money than Chuck's mom did since his dad wasn't paying for him to take the bus to school.

Living seven long blocks from the school, I thought I lived farther than any kid who walked to school. In fact, some kids who lived closer to the school than I did took the bus. Of course, if I had a bus pass, I would only be able to use it after school since there was no school bus before 8 o'clock in the morning when I'd be headed to school with Sue for band rehearsal. Anyway, students who lived farther away from school than I did usually took the bus or were driven to school by someone. The blocks between my house and the school seemed to be very long, and there were no sidewalks on Rose Avenue. Therefore, Sue and I had to walk on the street. Sometimes I felt embarrassed when the school bus passed me walking home from school and the kids on the bus saw me carrying all my books, music folder, and clarinet case. When I wasn't staying after school for an activity, I sometimes took my time leaving the school grounds just so the bus would go down Rose Avenue before I would walk home. That way, nobody on the bus would see me and be reminded that I didn't get to take the bus. It was interesting, if not comforting, to know that Tim walked farther than my sister and me. This made me feel good to know that not everybody got a ride that far except us. As they say, misery loves company.

Actually, when the weather was really bad, one teacher or another would sometimes stop and offer us a ride as we walked to band in the morning because some of the teachers drove down our street on their way to school. One of them was a neighbor and a good friend of my mom's. She was my teacher in second grade. The other one was a nice older man who taught eighth grade and was one of the coaches.

Before getting a drink of water at the water faucet down my classroom's hallway, Tim invited me back to the parking lot, his hideout, anytime I might hate my class again. I told him, "I'll see you again real soon if they treat me like they did this morning." Going further down the hallway to my classroom, I couldn't figure out why Tim hated his classmates so much but seemed to want to talk to me. Again, this made me wonder what was wrong with me. Why would an anti-social kid like me but nobody else?

When I got back in the classroom, there was a crowd of students around my desk. They were excitedly up to something. I was torn between wanting to run back to hide in the parking lot, which I couldn't do, and walking through the crowd, which I had to do to get to my desk. When I got there, the students jumped back. Some of them had guilty looks and others laughed deviously. They had scribbled all over my Nixon signs. Only the very bottom of the first N in Nixon's name was still visible on one of the two signs. The other one was totally torn to shreds. Crayon, pencil, and pen marks crossed everything out. My desk was a total mess. Everyone waited for my reaction, but my shyness refused to allow me to give one. I turned to Miss McCauley for a look of sympathy, at least. I got none. Her big round face was showing a smile like I'd rarely seen on her face. I turned to Chuck. He had his usual smile, showing his bright white teeth. Though I couldn't see his eyes through his long dirty blonde hair, which usually hung down over his eyes like a shaggy dog's hair, I could see the creases along the sides of his eyes. The creases always formed when he made a big smile or laughed. When I turned to Ray, he was kneeling on his seat, yelling, "Ya lousy Nixon supporter. Why don't ya go to Russia and take Nixon with ya?" I expected it from Ray because I knew he could be a jerk when he wanted to be. I had found at times that he was the type of kid who would kick you when you were down. But I was kind of disappointed in Chuck. Though he was only smiling and not laughing at me or yelling insults at me, I thought he would lay low and not join in with the others who were making me feel bad.

In spite of the laughter, I could sense the tremendous dislike many of these students had for me just because I had appeared to be a Nixon supporter. I couldn't imagine being treated like this just because, on the surface, I didn't agree with their choice for president. The fact that I really wasn't for Nixon didn't matter. I figured that if I had told the truth, that I was really for Kennedy but made a Nixon sign to keep peace at my house and to satisfy my mom, hardly anyone would have believed me. Worse yet, they would have just thought I was a momma's boy by making the sign my mom wanted me to make. I hated the term mama's boy, but I caught myself being one this time. Anyway, I never explained any of this to anyone in the class. I was being labeled a Nixon supporter for life and would have to live with it.

I was thinking that I would likely end up in the "D" row if Miss McCauley disliked Nixon as much as Mom disliked Kennedy. However, my worries about what Miss McCauley thought were replaced with terrific anger when I saw that students had gone in my desk and scribbled dirty words and insulting names on my notebooks and textbooks. If Miss McCauley had seen the names, she probably wouldn't have found all of this so humorous since most of the names fit her physical appearance. I thought that either Miss McCauley or Chuck should have tried to stop the class from getting so carried away with their hatred of my alleged Nixon support. Since neither of them did, I was disappointed in both of them, especially Chuck. I thought he was a best friend. Well, live and learn. I also lost some of the respect I had for my teacher because stopping the students' cruel actions would have been the right thing for a teacher to do.

Election Day wasn't quite as hard as the previous day. Yet, by appearing to be for Nixon, I was different from everyone else in my classroom, and I was treated like a freak for it. It seemed so strange to me that it was this presidential election assignment, the making of the signs, which made me first hear prejudiced comments from Mom. Through this, I realized how much I hated even thinking that people would be treated badly simply because they were different or had different opinions. Then, ironically, I was the one experiencing prejudice. All I could do for now, and hopefully forever, would be to ignore prejudiced people as best I could. To think that all of this began with the misunderstanding that my class really thought I wanted Vice President Nixon to become the next president. After all this, I didn't know what to think anymore. If the kids in my class and Miss McCauley were representative of the kinds of people who supported Kennedy, maybe I shouldn't have been a Kennedy supporter after all. I certainly wasn't like these supporters of his. There was no way that I could relate to their prejudiced actions. Though I still kind of wanted Kennedy to win for the same reasons as before, I now wouldn't have minded nearly as much if he would lose. If Nixon were to win, I'd kind of be getting even with the class and Miss McCauley for all of the harassment I had been receiving.

That afternoon, I stayed with Tim in the parking lot again. I told him all about the morning events in my classroom. He agreed that my classmates were being jerks by destroying my signs and invading my privacy when they went in my desk. He came up with some ways of getting even with my teacher and classmates for the way they were treating me. However, they involved breaking into the school at night and doing other illegal things. Therefore, I just thanked him for his suggestions while knowing I would never do the things he had suggested. He went as far as suggesting I poison them. Anyway, after recess, I went to the gymnasium with the other band kids to prepare for the assembly. The other kids who weren't in the band followed us to the gym about fifteen minutes later. As the students who weren't in the band entered the gymnasium, we were playing one march after another. We played *Semper Fidelis, You're a Grand*

Old Flag, and my very favorite which is called *Colonel Bogey March*. Next, Principal Monge turned on the microphone and talked about American's freedoms. Then he said how we should all exercise our right to vote when we are old enough to do so.

Mr. Monge also spoke about both presidential candidates. Though he didn't come right out and admit it, I sensed that he was for Nixon, just like my mom. He said that Nixon served the country well as President Eisenhower's Vice President for the past eight years and had definitely paid his dues to become the nation's new leader. When some students booed his complements about Nixon, he got angry. Well, not angry compared to other adults, but angry for Mr. Monge. He really wasn't the type of person who ever got very mad about much of anything. Then he spoke about the admirable ambitions of young John Fitzgerald Kennedy. He gave a brief history of the man, including the fact that he was more than just a senator from Massachusetts but also a past member of the House of Representatives. I knew he was a senator, but I didn't know he was a former representative as well. Until this talk by Mr. Monge, I didn't know that Kennedy had also written a book called *Profiles in Courage* that had won a Pulitzer Prize. He said a few things about him that I already knew, such as Kennedy becoming the youngest President ever elected if he were to win. Mr. Monge also told us that Kennedy would become the first Catholic president if he were to win. The fact that Kennedy was Catholic was probably why many of the kids at my school were for him instead of Nixon. The neighborhoods around the school were predominantly Catholic.

For the rest of the principal's talk, I sat there wondering if everybody in my class was Catholic except me. This seemed possible since most kids talked about going to catechism on Saturday mornings. From what I had heard, catechism was sort of like my Sunday school, but it was for Catholics instead of Protestants and held on Saturday instead of Sunday. As I had these thoughts, my feeling of being alone and being discriminated against became more pronounced. I was beginning to think that maybe there was more to the Nixon versus Kennedy thing than I had first realized. Maybe, by crossing Nixon's name off my desk, they actually were meaning to cross off the word Protestant. If this had been a Catholic versus Protestant thing all along, this is a battle I would never win in my classroom due to the numbers. Not only were all the kids most likely Catholic, but I knew Miss McCauley was also Catholic because the kids that attended the nearby Catholic church had mentioned seeing her at their church. How rude, I thought, that the class would shame me for not being their religion, if that's what they were doing. Again, this was a prejudice of which I didn't want to experience. Therefore, I tried to erase the thought and put my mind back on the assembly.

When the principal asked the Nixon supporters to take center floor in the gymnasium, the masses of Kennedy supporters booed again. Some yelled the word commie, which was a derogatory slang word for Communist. To that, the principal loudly and firmly said, "If there is any more booing or disrespect for either presidential candidate, we will all be going back to class for a lengthy lesson in proper behavior and respect. One of these fine men will soon be our president. I suggest you think about that." Again, Mr. Monge was not one to get mad, but he was clearly irritated. Likely due to the threat of having to go back to class, the booing stopped.

Out of those hundreds of kids in our school, there were only about twenty-five of us out on the floor, marching in a huge sparse circle with our Nixon posters. Besides my sister, the only other person I knew well on the floor was Murph. He marched close to my sister and me. That gym floor never seemed as big as it did right then. None too soon, the principal thanked us for our display of patriotism and then said, "Now, the Nixon supporters will return to their seats and make room for the Kennedy supporters." The thunderous burst of applause, cheering, and moving feet was deafening as the students came down from the bleachers to the floor. Mr. Mattei yelled, "Stars and Stripes." With most of the band members on the gymnasium floor to show their support for Kennedy, there were few band members still sitting in front of Mr. Mattei. Yet, my sister, one drummer, a few other band members, and I started playing the march while the crowd was marching around the packed floor. But the enthusiastic crowd of Kennedy supporters drowned us out. So, Mr. Mattei just waved his arms, motioning us to stop. We watched the pandemonium. As the students marching around the gym floor were becoming too enthusiastic, Mr. Monge took the microphone and said, "Now, teachers, let's guide the students back to the bleachers." After a brief pause he continued, "No, better yet, let's guide them down the hall and back to their classrooms. Single file, of course." Since the assembly was obviously over, I started putting my instrument away. Everyone remained in the classrooms for the last half-hour of the day before the final bell sounded.

That afternoon, Murph came to basketball practice. The coach told him that he was glad to see him coming out because, he explained, "Sports are good for disciplining any young man." Due to Murph's reputation, which he had earned from hanging around with a circle of tough guys, the coach probably thought he needed disciplining. As the coach walked away, Murph turned to me, gave me his big smile, and quietly said, "He won't be so glad when he sees me shoot the ball." This first practice with Murph was great since we only had to run a few laps around the gym and shoot layups for a short while. We spent the rest of the time talking on the bench since the coach needed time to work with the first string for a big game, which was to be played in a few days.

Murph and I talked about how uncomfortable we were to be practically the only Nixon supporters on the gym floor that afternoon. He surprised me when he said that his family was probably the only Catholic family around that wanted Nixon to win. When he said why his mom wanted Kennedy to lose, it was like hearing my mother's reasons all over again. Before we left practice, the coach called Murph, the other benchwarmers, and me over to the far wall to have a chat while the good players headed for the locker room. He usually only had chats with his better players. However, this talk was for everybody else. He told us that basketball was good for disciplining our minds and keeping our bodies fit, and he said that he was glad that we came out for the sport. After the nice talk, he laid it on the line by saying, "Soon, gentlemen, I'll be working exclusively with my regular first and second string. I've got some big conference games coming up which Chaney School's basketball team needs to win. Chaney needs to uphold its fine reputation of being the home of winners. So, sometime between Thanksgiving break and Christmas break, I'll be making final cuts. In other words, fellas, you've got to show me that you're a basketball player who is a benefit to the team, or you won't need to stay for practice for more than a few more weeks. If being on the team is important to you and you practice every day like some of the boys do, you'll have a better chance of making the final cut. It's up to you." So, I knew that in a month or so, there'd be no need for me to have to stay after school for basketball practice. I wasn't motivated to practice basketball every day because making the team was definitely not important to me. As we headed across the gym floor for the locker room, he added, "Oh, fellas, let your parents know, too, so they won't be surprised when the day comes." Some parents probably argued if their boy didn't make the team. Somehow, I knew my parents didn't expect me to make it anyway. There was apparently no way Murph would make the final cut either. During his first practice, he was as non-athletic as he said he was.

On the way home from practice Murph said that even if he did make the team, he probably wouldn't be on the team until the end of the season anyway. He said his dad might be transferred over the Christmas vacation, in about seven weeks, and they would probably start looking for a house on the North Side of Chicago so his dad wouldn't have to travel far to get to work. I said, "Aw, you're kidding me, Murph!" I surprised myself with my open disappointment. After a lengthy silence, he said, "But my dad said this once before a couple of years ago and we didn't move anywhere. So maybe I won't move this time either. My ma and I will just have to wait and see. Dad calls the shots." I was hoping that he wasn't just saying this to give me false hope that he wouldn't move. When I got home, I was quieter than usual. Mom asked what was wrong, and I just said that I was tired. I didn't even want to talk about the possibility of Murph moving away. And even if I did, she probably would have told me that I shouldn't let it bother me since there would be nothing I could do about it. I never liked hearing that the things that troubled me shouldn't bother me. Obviously, the possibility of Murph moving bothered me a lot. I mean, talk about bad luck! I finally had a friend that I could really talk to about most anything, and he might leave town just months after I'd struck up a friendship with him. It seemed so unfair, but there was nothing I could do about it. I thought about only having Ray and Chuck as friends again, and it made me feel worse. I knew I couldn't have those serious, grown-up kinds of talks with them because Ray was too private and Chuck wasn't mature enough yet.

That evening, the family ended up eating bowls of Neapolitan ice cream, which was one-third chocolate, one-third vanilla, and one-third strawberry, on TV trays in the living room as we watched the news coverage of the election returns. Recent polls showed that the vote tallies would be close. The commentators on television were predicting a long night. So, I forgot about going to bed to feel sorry for myself about Murph possibly leaving town and got interested in the election coverage. On television, they started talking about something called the Electoral College. They were saying that the Electoral College was what had to be won and not necessarily the people's vote total. With that, I became confused and disappointed. I thought the person who got the most votes would win the election. However, with the Electoral College that I had never heard of before, there was a catch. There was actually a chance that the politician with the most votes from the people could lose. I went to bed not knowing who won.

The morning after the election, just after Mom had gotten me up, I entered the living room and heard the television announcer say, "John Fitzgerald Kennedy, the forty-three year old senator from Massachusetts, will become the thirty-fifth president of these United States. The victory comes as a shock to the Nixon camp." Mom instructed me to scrape our Nixon sign off the storm window of the front door of our house. I dressed quickly so I could get it off before anyone would ride by and see me removing it. It took me quite a while to scrape it off with one of Dad's razor blades. As I was working away at it, a car went by, honking its horn repeatedly. When I looked, it was a car full of people, some of whom were pointing at the remnants of our Nixon sign and me. I didn't recognize anyone in the car, so I didn't care. At the breakfast table, Mom solemnly said, "People like your father are going to have to just keep working as hard as they can and pray for the best. Your father works all week at the office and then Friday nights and most Saturdays down at that store. Now the government will be taking more out of his checks in taxes just to give his hard-earned money to people who don't want to work." She was so upset that she was visibly shaking.

When Sue and I got to school, some kids were just finding out about the Kennedy victory. They were overjoyed, to say the least. I expected a few snide remarks from my classmates, but they left me alone. Besides, our teacher gave us so much work to complete by morning recess that no one had time to bother anybody. During recess, I visited Tim in the parking lot. Though he seemed a bit unusual, I liked how he enjoyed talking to me. And he didn't talk about politics at all. I found that comforting and refreshingly different. Hopefully, with the election finally being over, everybody would quit talking about politics.

Chapter Thirteen: Fooling the Class Bully

The next night, I made a very bold move at my clarinet lesson. I decided that I would no longer hide my uniqueness, at least not from those who might appreciate it. After I played my clarinet lesson for Mr. Williamson, I took my latest song from the lining of my clarinet case and asked him what he thought of it. He held it in front of his face and stared at it. He said, "Hearing is believing. Play it for me." After I did, he didn't say that he liked it or not, but he said that he thought it was great that I was writing music. While I still had my courage up, I also took out *Walk – Don't Run*, which I had been keeping in my clarinet case, too. Though he didn't know the song by its title, he recognized it when I played it for him. Again, I could see that he was pleased that I had written it out and was able to play it for him. When Dad arrived to pick Sue and me up from our lessons, Mr. Williamson said, "He's really something, Mr. Paulson." I loved being complimented like this in front of my dad. I could think of nothing more satisfying than to see Dad being proud of me.

The four-day Thanksgiving weekend finally arrived. Everything was always cancelled during the long holiday weekend, and I looked forward to the free time without school or other activities. Thanksgiving had always been a fun day with the relatives and all the food at Grandma's house. This year was different, though, as Mom asked Grandma to join us at our house for the turkey, stuffing, mashed potatoes, sweet potatoes, and a variety of side dishes and desserts. Grandma said she would come. She also asked if all the people who usually had come to her house on past Thanksgivings could come, too. At that, people packed our house, and many of them brought food to help my mom out. As far as I could remember, we had never had so many people eating at our house. During the meal, Grandma seemed to be all right except for hardly being able to let ten minutes pass without mentioning Grandpa. It was depressing to see how much she was still missing him. I wondered if she would ever get over it. By now, I had hoped that she would be dealing with it better. Christmas was only about four weeks away, and I was starting to dread it since Grandma would probably be feeling down during the first Christmas without Grandpa, too.

During that long weekend, the family didn't do many of the things we normally did during that time of year, like begin Christmas shopping and looking at the holiday decorations in the stores and the ones that would already be displayed on city streets. Instead, we stayed home while Mom spent lots of time at Grandma's house. I wondered if holidays would ever be the same again. Since Thanksgiving seemed to be an emotional setback for Grandma and Mom, I wished there was a way to skip holidays until Grandma got over Grandpa's death. But maybe she never would.

That Sunday, we took Grandma to church and out to eat with us. As much as Grandma tried to act pleasant, she didn't seem happy. Adding an eeriness to it all, as we were taking Grandma back to her house, she said, "Someday, I'll be with Pa again." Nobody, not even Mom, knew what to say after that. The car was silent until we got to her house. For the first time, after this long weekend, I was almost glad to go back to school where everybody's minds and conversations would turn from turkeys and pilgrims to Christmas and presents. Even though I wasn't looking forward to our family's Christmas in the way I had in the past, I was determined to have fun watching everyone else's enthusiasm for the holiday season build at school.

I spent a lot of time during that long weekend in the basement with my clarinet. By the end of that weekend, I was playing many radio songs by ear. I didn't feel like writing new ones of my own. With Thanksgiving weekend over, I thought I'd try to spend more time after school at Murph's house. We were both anxious to play pool. Though he hadn't mentioned moving since he had said it back on Election Day, about three weeks ago, I was afraid to ask since I feared that moving was still a strong possibility. By now, I could say Murph had become my best friend. With the weather getting colder and Murph living closer to my house than Chuck did, I was seeing

Murph even more than I used to see Chuck. Ray still couldn't deal with more than one friend at a time, I guess, because he never came around when I was with Murph. I found this to be very peculiar. Yet, I liked not having Ray around because he insulted me more when he had an audience like Murph. Maybe he thought that by trying to make me look bad, he would make himself look better. Very different from Ray, Murph built my ego up by telling me things that made me feel good about myself. He'd tell me that I was good for him because I didn't smoke. He said it was tough to quit smoking, and I was helping him by being his one good friend who didn't smoke. When his other friends lit up, he said he always would too. Since I'd only had two puffs in my entire life, I couldn't understand a person's smoking addiction and how it could be so difficult for someone to quit. But he said it was tough to do and that I helped him by simply not smoking. He thought people who smoke should only smoke around other smokers because it bothers non-smokers' eyes. I agreed with him since smoke made my eyes tear up. Anyway, he never smoked around me again after that first time I had seen him smoke with Ray on Halloween night. I respected him for being so considerate of my eyes. I also had told him how my mom could smell smoke on my clothes after Halloween night, and he probably didn't want me to have to go through that again. He was considerate.

The week after Thanksgiving, I received the second report card for the 1960-61 school year. I was delighted to see that my grades stayed about the same. In fact, one of my grades somehow improved. My seat stayed the same, though. I still sat in the fourth desk in the "A" row. In fact, the entire first row stayed the same. The only bad thing about the new grading period's seating arrangement was that Chuck moved up to the front of the "B" row. Though I was happy to see him look and feel proud for having moved up, I selfishly didn't like that he no longer sat across from me. In fact, I rather felt sorry for him because his desk was right up front by Miss McCauley. He wouldn't be able to get away with anything with her sitting so close to him.

One of the notorious fifth-grade bullies, David, now sat across from me. Everyone knew that David made kids show him their answers. He was a cheater. If he hadn't cheated, he probably would have been somewhere in the "D" row. Except for some of the teachers at Chaney, I think practically everybody knew David was a poor reader. Yet, in spite of his reputation for being a bully, I didn't plan on giving him any answers. David, however, didn't know of my plan and started pushing my elbow out of his eye's view of my paper the very first day I had to sit by him. The more I acted irritated by his dishonest actions, the more persistent he was in his effort to look at my paper. Though telling Miss McCauley about his attempt to cheat crossed my mind, I knew I wouldn't tell because I never was a tattletale at school. Plus, David probably would have beat me up. I would only tattle on my siblings at home, especially Brett, because they ratted on me sometimes. But as irritated as David made me, I knew I'd have to do something for my own peace of mind.

The next Friday, Miss McCauley gave the class two tests. One was in history and the other was in mathematics. I thought David would definitely want to see my papers during the tests. I was right. Tired of having my elbow pushed off my papers, I didn't bother to hide them. First, the class was given the history test, which consisted of twenty true and false questions. Unlike most history tests I had taken in earlier years in school, I'd studied for this one because grades were important to me in this class. With extreme confidence, I read the first of the twenty sentences and put true, the correct answer, on the blank before the sentence. Next, I read the second sentence, and I wrote the word false, the wrong answer, on the space before the sentence. Next, I wrote false, the correct answer, for number three. Then, I wrote true, the wrong answer, for number four. I continued putting the correct answers for all of the odd-numbered statements until I got to number nineteen. I put the incorrect answers for all of the even-numbered statements. Knowing that David was still watching my paper, I wrote Scott Paulson in my best cursive handwriting in the upper right-hand corner and sat while looking over my answers. As David got up to turn his paper in, I quickly changed all of my true even-numbered answers to false and my false even-numbered answers to true. When David returned to his seat, I was still changing the last couple of even-numbered answers. He grumbled, "What are you doing?" Miss McCauley yelled, "Quiet over there!" I didn't respond to David, especially since the teacher had yelled for it to get quiet. Then I turned my paper in.

Unfortunately, this did not deter David from looking at my math test later in the day, though. The test was on long division. I not only was good at long division, but I enjoyed working with numbers in any way, shape, or form. Again, I had a plan for David's roaming eyes. For the first ten division problems, I wrote the correct answers on the test. After that, however, I began writing some incorrect answers. For the remainder of the test, I added one to the answer's number for every odd numbered problem on the test. Number eleven on the test was to solve 1,049 divided by 7. Instead of putting 149 remainder 6, the correct answer, I added one to the answer and wrote 150 remainder 6. I used this method of writing the wrong answers for all of the odd-numbered math problems through the last math problem, number 25. When I was finished, I wrote my name in the upper right-hand corner and looked at my test paper as if I were rechecking my work. Eventually, David turned in his paper before most other students, likely in an effort to look smart again. That's when I began changing my wrong answers to their correct answers by simply taking one number off the answers I had answered incorrectly on purpose. Though he must have seen me making changes, he didn't say anything to me this time. Yes, it was extra work for me, but it was fun work since I was on a mission to keep this kid from cheating off me. Worse than a cheater, he was a bully, too. Therefore, I did not want to help him get a good grade dishonestly.

After I dusted eraser crumbs off my paper, I mentally calculated that David had eight incorrect answers on his test of 25 math problems. His grade would be 68 percent when 70 percent was needed to pass. As long as he would never know for sure whether I was tricking him or not, he likely wouldn't take revenge. I wanted him to think that I wasn't as smart as he thought and that I had to change my mind often before finally turning my papers in. Regardless of what he thought, my plan apparently worked because, from that day on, he copied off the girl in front of him, Sherry, instead. He kept his big eyes off my papers. Seeing this cheater fail two tests, thanks to me, was extremely satisfying because he was one of the most verbally abusive students in the classroom during my two disastrous Nixon days during the presidential election. At a young age, I learned that, when justified, revenge can be sweet.

Chapter Fourteen: Anticipating Christmas

The weeks of school between Thanksgiving and Christmas break went by fast again. Actually, some referred to the time off at the end of the school year as the winter break. But most of us called it Christmas break. There was always so much to do during the holiday season. The demanding band practices as well as the band performances for the students at the school assembly and for our parents at the evening program kept me very busy. For the most part, I practiced legitimately during those weeks because I had a big solo in one of the Christmas songs that I didn't want to mess up. I knew I'd be nervous about having a solo in front of all those people and thought I'd be less nervous if I was over-rehearsed. As I would have to do at the Christmas concerts, I practiced it while standing in the basement at our house. I made myself memorize the solo too, because I thought I would look more talented and confident without needing to look at music sitting on a music stand. I really wanted my parents, siblings, classmates, and all the teachers to be impressed as well as proud of me. Building quite a reputation for myself as a clarinet player, I just had to work hard at doing my best on this opportunity that Mr. Mattei was giving me by letting me perform a solo.

The teachers, including Miss McCauley, always had special activities in the classroom during December. We spent hours making Christmas decorations for the classroom and the hallway outside of our classroom. Of the jobs available for decorating, I preferred helping make the green and red paper chains, which we would hang from one long fluorescent light fixture to the next across the classroom's ceiling. The kids who were apparently best at doing artwork cut out a big tree for the decoration that was taped on the hallway's side of our classroom door. Then, everyone in the class made a small paper ornament to paste on the paper tree. I made a blue ornament since blue is my favorite color. In each grade, the students in the classroom with the nicest door decoration, as determined by Mr. Monge, would get an extra gym period and some treats before the Christmas vacation. I was never in a class that won the competition, and from the looks of the decorations this year, I still wasn't going to be part of a winning classroom. The tree our class made wasn't big enough for the huge door and it wasn't shaped quite right. It looked more like a decorated egg standing upright than a tree.

We also wrote Christmas poems and used them for the insides of Christmas cards we made for our parents and other people. I think everyone in our entire class, if not the entire school, was Christian even though we went to different types of churches. Therefore, I don't think anyone would have complained about doing Christmas activities in December. With the red and green paper Miss McCauley provided, I made cards for Mom, Dad, Sue, Brett, Grandma, Chuck, and Murph. Even though Ray went to church and catechism, he was vocal about letting me know that he didn't like making or exchanging Christmas cards. Therefore, he only made cards for his parents. Consequently, since he didn't think Christmas cards were cool to give or get, I didn't make him one. However, even with his different attitude toward Christmas cards, I hoped he would have a merry Christmas anyway. When I saw kids making cards for Miss McCauley, I thought it was a nice idea, and I made her one. Some kids gave her cards before the last day before Christmas break. She placed them on her desk, facing the class. After some students said that these kids were just trying to be the teacher's pet, I hid the card I had made for her in my desk. I planned to put it on her desk, face down, late in the afternoon on the last day of school before the vacation started. I wouldn't mind being one of her pet students, but I certainly wouldn't want anyone to know I made moves to be one.

The night before the last day of school before Christmas break, the band performed the Christmas concert for our families and anyone else who wanted to come. I was surprised to see that I was much more relaxed performing my solo for adults than I was that afternoon when I played it in the school assembly with all the students and teachers in grades one through eight watching me. I had read that it is good to look at the wall behind the audience if seeing faces makes a performer nervous. In spite of planning to do that, I forgot and looked right at Mr. Mattei while playing the solo at both performances. Thank God, I did a respectable job at both performances and got a nice round of applause, especially at the evening performance.

After we got home from the concert, Mom once again asked Dad to reach far up into the top shelf of the cupboard cabinets to get the cookie cutters that made the various shapes of Christmas cookies. After Mom washed the metal contraptions off, we made green cookies in the shape of Christmas trees and sprinkled red and white speckles on them as they cooled off on the cookie sheets. Mom wrapped most of the cookies up on paper plates. Since the left over cookies didn't last long at our house, Mom would hide some from us so that there would be some for anyone who might visit over the holidays. Dad's brothers always stopped by during this time of year, and sometimes Mom's sister would visit with her husband and kids. Besides these possible visitors, Dad always saved a few for the mailman, the kid who brought the newspaper to our house every day, and for Santa on Christmas Eve. Since Brett was still just a little kid, Dad continued putting cookies and milk out for Santa every Christmas Eve. I figured this would continue until Brett got in the second grade. After all, that was the year Mom told me what I had already known. I figured it out long before I went to school but played along for Brett's sake and, more importantly, to ensure that I'd still get gifts from Santa.

Anyway, on the day before Christmas break began at school, Mom gave Sue, Brett, and me our packages of Christmas cookies for our three teachers and Mr. Mattei. Even though I think I liked Mr. Mattei more than Sue did, I let her give him his plate of cookies. I decided to give Miss McCauley her card and the plate of cookies during afternoon recess when very few kids would see me doing it. Again, I didn't want to look like I was trying to become a teacher's pet by letting the entire class see me gift her. Though being called a teacher's pet wasn't as bad as being called other nicknames like Fatso, I preferred getting through the last school day of the calendar year without being called any names at all. The next school day would be on January 2, 1961. The best present anyone could possibly give me was the vacation the school gave. I would be able to stay up later than usual, and I wouldn't have to get up at seven o'clock in the morning for the next nine days unless I wanted to do so.

Chapter Fifteen: Christmas

A week before the first day of the Christmas vacation was on a Saturday, eight days before Christmas. Dad took Brett and me to buy a Christmas tree at the lot behind a grocery store on Jefferson Street, which was on the west side of Joliet. We had bought groceries at this store many times. We went tree shopping late in the afternoon because Dad worked at the store until 5:00 on this particular Saturday. He usually didn't work there that late throughout the year, but they gave him more hours during December because the store was exceptionally busy right before Christmas. At the Christmas tree lot, Brett and I found a big, full tree and tried to persuade Dad to buy it. But with his typical style of humor, Dad said, "It'll look funny with the top cut off, won't it?" That is when I realized that the tree was too tall to fit in our living room. Even though our house had high ceilings, this tree was too tall for it. So, the three of us found a shorter one. Brett and I watched the salesman and Dad tie it to the top of our car after Dad paid for it. Then we slowly drove back roads to get back home. At home, we went in the living room and found that Mom and Sue had cleared the corner where we always put the tree. Dad and I carried it into the house and put it in the water stand. As Dad had other years, he was cautious and put the tree a good distance from the radiator that poured out heat throughout the winter months. He told me that if he wouldn't have done so, it could have caused a fire. Even if it hadn't caused a fire, the pines would have fallen off the tree before Christmas. Mom once told me that one year, at another house they lived in before I was born, they put the tree too close to heat, and when they went to bed at night they could hear the pines fall off the tree onto the wooden floor of the house.

Next, we decked the tree with electric colored lights from branch to branch. To top things off, Dad perched an angel on the top of the tree. Separating and hanging the tinsel, strand by strand, was usually my job. Though I didn't like the boring, time-consuming job at all, every year I was told that I was very good at it and, therefore, did it without fussing. Was I naïve or what? Anyway, all of our work was worth it when the tree was finished because it would look nice. Dad would also lay a white cotton cloth, embedded with silver speckles, around the foot of the tree. On the cloth, we would arrange the manger scene with the clay figures of Jesus in the manger, Mary, Joseph, and the three wise men. There were also figures of camels, one of which had the front left leg broken off. I don't know when or how it broke, but it must have been many years ago, maybe before I was born, because I always remembered that camel being without one of its legs. The three-legged camel stood fine if no one touched it, but the slightest motion would make it topple over. Finally, we would hang our Christmas stockings from the edge of our fake fireplace. I found it unusual that we had a fireplace that wouldn't really burn logs and wouldn't heat the living room, but Mom wanted one so much that we had a fake.

Dad always decorated our yard, too. As I got older, Dad accumulated more outdoor decorations. He made all of the Christmas decorations except for the store-bought strings of colored lights, which he attached to the rain gutters around the roof's edge of the house. It took many lights to stretch around our huge house. The decorations he made looked better than the things sold in stores. By this Christmas, our house was by far the most decorated house in our neighborhood. I was always very proud of Dad and our house, especially when people would stop their cars in front of our house to look. Many people peered out of their windows to treat their eyes to Dad's festive handy work. A few times, I even saw people get out of their cars and take pictures.

Dad's wooden figures of Santa's reindeer as well as Santa's sleigh, which was packed with Santa and colorful packages, stretched halfway across the front yard. He also had five snowmen, or should I say three wooden snowmen and two wooden snow-ladies. With black paint, he'd painted all our names on them. The largest snowman said Dad, the next largest which was a snow-lady said Mom, the middle-sized one said Sue, the next one was for me and said Scott, and the smallest one said Brett. Dad's was holding a huge sign that said: Merry Christmas from the Paulson Family. At night, several bright spotlights, which Dad had positioned in front of them, lit up all the decorations. Every year the decorations would just seem to appear. This particular year, Dad put up everything except the lights while we kids were sleeping early on a Sunday morning before Christmas. In all of the years that he put the decorations out in the yard, I only remember seeing him put the colored lights up on the trim of the house. This year, like last, Mom sent me out to hold the ladder steady to make sure he wouldn't fall. I really think he loved doing this for us every year. And I'm glad he did because it made our house very special during the Christmas season.

When Christmas Eve day arrived this year, Mom and Dad took us to Woolworth's discount store downtown. With the money I was given, I would find a gift for everyone in the family and Grandma. At the discount store, this was easy to do. In fact, I could usually get Mom and Dad two things because of the money I'd have left over. This particular year, I bought Dad some socks and shaving cream, and I got Mom a white apron and some stuff that ladies put on their face. I bought a Brenda Lee record for Sue, a coffee mug for Grandma, and some little plastic soldiers for Brett. He liked lining things up on the bedroom's hardwood floor and playing with them like I did when I was his age. Probably because I was determined to get Mom and Dad two gifts each, I figured that with tax I didn't have quite enough money. I borrowed a little more from Dad and gave it back as soon as we got home. In my closet, I had a huge piggy bank with change in it. Dad and one of my uncles, Dad's brother, often gave me change for no reason at all. It was difficult to shake the coins out, but with some patience, it could be done when I needed money. I figured that since Dad was good enough to give me money to buy everybody gifts, it would be stingy of me to expect more than the amount I was given without paying him back.

I always knew that most everyone would be buying me something related to food or music. After all, those were the things everyone knew I'd want the most. A 45-rpm record and a boxed Chef Boyardee Pizza, which I liked making and eating by myself, were usually all I had on my Christmas list. Any other things I thought of, like a new clarinet or my own TV, would have cost too much money. I knew the gifts on my list were reasonable requests because the pizza cost less than a dollar even with tax at the grocery store on Jefferson Street and a 45-rpm record was only 69 cents plus tax down at Polk Brother's record department. This year, the records I wanted were the instrumental songs, the ones without words. I liked those songs the most. The few times I got records I didn't want, I kept them anyway because I'd always want to remember who chose which record for me.

Back at home, we went to our own rooms and wrapped the gifts. Since Brett and I shared a room, we didn't worry about how we wrapped one another's gifts. We just showed one another what we'd bought and got some paper around it fast. We both hated to wrap, and this way we would each have one less gift that we needed to wrap with care. Besides, he always bought me a record, and it would have been pretty hard for him to disguise it like Sue always did. Last year, he got me a record and wrapped it. After he fell asleep, I unwrapped it and then put the wrapping back on it because I was anxious to see what he got me. I did that with some of the gifts under the tree, too. Some years I knew what Sue was getting before she even knew because I snooped if any of her gifts looked like a record. Even though it wouldn't be mine, I wanted to know what record she would be playing in the house on and after Christmas Day. Sue was the most creative gift wrapper in the family. No one really knew what she'd bought for anyone until the gifts from her were unwrapped. I never snooped in gifts she wrapped and gave because it would be hard for me to put the wrapping back on the way she had it. Even though I pretty much knew the small gifts I'd be getting under the tree, there were always a couple of surprises. There would be a so-called surprise gift of a shirt, pants, some underwear, or socks under the tree. I didn't like those gifts, of course, but they were things I'd need for dressing nicely for school and church. Then, every year, Mom and Dad would get each of us kids one big gift, too. I usually got something I never even thought of asking for, but I loved it when I got it.

On Christmas Eve, we got ready for church. It was weird going to church on a Saturday evening since our church only had services on Sunday morning throughout the rest of the year. It would be fun at church, too, because the service would be nothing but music and the minister's telling of the Christmas story again. Sue and I were in the children's choir, so we performed on Christmas Eve. Though I didn't like singing in public, the church choir was okay. Besides, no one would know if I was faking it or not. Often, I just moved my mouth to the words because I didn't like the sound of my singing voice in the high range. The high range is where the songs were performed most of the time in the children's choir. My vocal range was lower than the average kid's voice. So I'd spare the ears of the people around me, as well as my own, and just pretend to sing some of the time. After church, we began our traditional ride through the city's neighborhoods to look at the houses' decorations. The snow flurries that were falling throughout most of the day were still coming down. Though it wasn't nearly as cold as it was the past few days, it was still cold out with temperatures in the 20s. Since it was cold and snow was lightly coming down, Mom wanted to cancel the ride for this year and go straight home. Sensing our disappointment, Dad quietly told her, "We can't do that, Hon. The kids look forward to this every year." Mom said, "All right, but if we have an accident, it'll ruin Christmas." Dad assured her that the roads weren't that bad and that we wouldn't have an accident. "And besides," he reasoned with her, "there are hardly any other cars on the road to have an accident with." At that, she sat quietly biting her bottom lip as she often did when she was concerned. During our ride, we went past the houses that were the first, second, and third place winners in the local newspaper's annual Christmas decorations' contest. Mom, who now appeared to have become as relaxed as the rest of us, noted that the winning decorations were usually in the wealthier neighborhoods of the city and were usually store-bought decorations. It seemed unfair that they didn't list Dad's as the winner because it was obvious to me that his decorations were better than any others we had seen again this Christmas Eve. I wondered if the judges of the contest from the newspaper even looked at decorations in our neighborhood. After all, our neighborhood was a distance from downtown Joliet. Regardless of who won, though, it was interesting to see how others decorated their houses for the holidays.

Back at home, we put our pajamas on, opened one gift from Mom and Dad, and then went to bed. I think Mom always gave me a clothing gift box on Christmas Eve so that I would have the gifts I really wanted on Christmas Day. This year I got a pair of blue jeans and a sports shirt in the clothing box. Mom said, "You'll like the gifts you're getting tomorrow more, Scott." Perhaps she could tell that I was less than pleased with gifts of clothes. Just before we kids went to bed, like on other Christmas Eves, Dad put a small plate with several Christmas cookies on it, a glass of milk, and a folded napkin on the ledge of the fireplace for Santa. After going to bed, I listened to hear what Mom and Dad were up to in the living room. Since my ears weren't too plugged up from the cold winter weather, I could hear their footsteps going from the basement to the living room. They must have hid the gifts in the locked coal room again. From the sound of it, someone was going to get something that moved on wheels. I was too old for a wagon and I already had a decent bicycle, so I figured that gift wasn't for me.

On Christmas morning, I woke up just before seven o'clock to the sound of Brett's quiet commotion in the other room. When I walked out of the bedroom and crossed the hall to the living room, he excitedly whispered, "Santa's been here, Scott!" He pointed to the top of the fireplace and said, "Look! He drank all the milk but left part of a cookie. Guess he didn't like 'em, huh?" As I finished Santa's cookies, I said, "Of course he liked them. But to be polite, he has to taste treats at every house that offers them. So he just samples a little and moves on to the next house. Otherwise, he'd get too full." He seemed to accept my excuse and then wanted to know if I thought the bicycle with the big red bow on the handlebars was for him or me. It was obviously a boy's bike, not for Sue, because the center bar was straight across from just below the handlebars' intersection to just below the seat. It was also obvious to me that it was for him because it was smaller than the bike I already had. I already had a twenty-four inch bike, and this one was probably only a twelve-inch.

Just then, I heard the toilet flush. I looked toward the open entrance to the hall and saw Sue joining us. She asked, "Brett, do you like the bicycle Santa brought you?" "Yeah," he said, "if it's really for me." Sue looked at me and whispered, "Did they forget to put his name on it?" Not wanting Brett to hear her, I said, "Shhh, Sue-Sue." But in the midst of Brett's excitement, he wasn't paying attention to her anyway. Then she told Brett, "It's your size, so it's got to be for you."

Soon thereafter, Mom and Dad came in. Mom said we should wait until she made coffee for Dad and herself before opening presents. We compromised. Mom started perking the Hills Bros., and then she came right back so that we could start opening our big gifts. I got a transistor radio with a 9-volt battery. "Do you like it?" asked everyone. "Yeah," I said, "it's just like Sue's except mine is black and newer!" I took it out of the box, and then Dad showed me how to put in the battery. I ran over to Sue and said, "Show me where WJOL is!" She said, "Nobody listens to that station." After a pause, she added, "Except old people." I knew of WJOL rather than the hit music station because it was the local radio station, and I had seen advertisements for it around town and had heard people mention it. As I turned red due to my embarrassment from being so terribly uncool, I asked, "What radio station do you listen to in your room all the time?" As she reached for my transistor, she said, "It's WLS, 8-9-0 on the dial. I'll find it for you." I thought, of course! W, L, and S were the letters printed across the top of the Silver Dollar Survey that I got at Polk Brothers record department every week after my music lesson. Dad jokingly interjecting, "Some of us old people listen to WLS, too." Then he informed, "The station just started playing the music you like last May. Before that, it was another one of those stations for old people."

That morning, the station was playing many Christmas songs. I really didn't care what they were playing, though. I just left the dial set to the station she said was the good one so that I wouldn't lose it and have to ask her to find it again. Like my phonograph, I played it with the volume turned all the way up. Dad was quick to show me how to use the plastic earplug, and he insisted I use it or turn the volume down. I used the earplug so I could blast the radio's volume.

After everyone opened their gifts, we had scrambled eggs and toast for breakfast. No one could believe I loved ketchup on my scrambled eggs, but I did, especially when we were out of American cheese. Then, we put the relatives' gifts, which Mom had bought and wrapped earlier in the month, in the back of the car and went to Grandma's house. This is where all the relatives on my mom's side of the family always gathered on Christmas Day. When we got there, at about eleven o'clock, everyone else had apparently arrived. Grandma always wanted everyone to be there by noon so that all of us grandchildren could open our gifts together without having to wait too long. The gift-giving procedure was the same every year. Grandma and Grandpa had bought a gift for everyone and each family bought a gift for each of them. Naturally, there was no gift exchanging with Grandpa this year, just Grandma. In addition, each child got a gift from each of the families. Though there was always talk of this being too much gift buying and exchanging, it never changed. Every year, Grandma's living room was filled with gifts to be opened, and I loved it.

As expected, everyone gave me a 45-rpm record except Grandma. She gave me a shirt with a color-matching sweater. Later, she went to the kitchen and came back with a small, somewhat heavy, wrapped gift and a brown paper bag. She said, "I think you'll like these better than those clothes your mother wanted me to give you." In the wrapped package was a small frying pan, and in the bag was a loaf of bread, a dozen eggs, a box of Velveeta cheese, and some bologna. Grandma smiled and said, "Now you can make your own sandwiches the way you like in your own frying pan." The adults knew I loved to make my own snacks and thought the gift was very thoughtful, but my brother, sister, and cousins laughed. I held the little black frying pan up in the air to remind them that I could do more than cook with it. Of course, I didn't hit anyone. My mom took the food items back to the kitchen to keep them refrigerated until we would head home.

Against my wishes, I went in Grandma's bathroom and tried the shirt and sweater on since Mom wanted to see if they fit me. I would have preferred going to the kitchen and trying out the frying pan with a couple slices of bread, butter, cheese, and bologna. Then while my cousins and my brother and sister played around with their gifts, I sat next to the radiator, listening to my transistor through the earpiece. Sue was right about WLS. It was terrific listening to *Walk – Don't Run*. By this time of day, on Christmas, the disc jockey had pretty much stopped playing the Christmas music and had started playing the hit records. I was used to hearing the songs filtered through my bedroom wall from Sue's room at home. Hearing them clearly through the radio and earpiece of the new transistor was much, much better. The records had so much more going on than just the voices and thumping rhythms I'd been hearing. On many songs, for the first time, I was hearing the total effect of the many instruments including the many guitars, keyboards, horns, violins and other sounds. It was awesome!

Including dinnertime at Grandma's, I didn't take the transistor's earpiece out of my ear all afternoon and evening. I started thinking about getting some more batteries before long because I was sure to run this one down real soon. Speaking of dinner, at Grandma's house, there was ham, which was one of my least favorite foods, her lumpy mashed potatoes, biscuits, some lettuce salad, and apple pies. I only ate a couple of biscuits, which I cut and smeared with butter, as well as a huge piece of apple pie. I thought it was Grandma doing most of the work in the kitchen, but I found out later that she had spent much of the day in her bedroom. So, Mom and my aunt must have done most of the cooking. I figured Grandma wasn't feeling well or was just too tired.

When we headed home in the car, I found out that if I held the transistor radio next to the window, it would still work without too much interference. Before that, all I'd hear in the car was lots of static sounds behind the songs. At home, I wanted to go in the basement and work out some of these songs on my clarinet, but Mom said it would be too cold and damp down there since the heat had been turned down all day while we were away. So instead, I just sat in the living room with everyone else and listened to my radio through the earpiece while everyone else watched television. Before long, however, I was watching television with them because I had already drained the battery that came with the radio. When I told Dad, he said that the battery that came with the radio was probably a cheap one. He said he would get me a new one tomorrow on his way home from work.

Since I didn't eat much at Grandma's house, I was getting hungry and asked Mom if I could try out my new frying pan with a couple of scrambled eggs and cheese. It was more fun to cook in my own frying pan that Grandma bought me. The eggs didn't have a chance to flatten out as much on the skillet since this pan was much smaller than Mom's was. I liked them better in the small one. After I washed everything up and found a place to put my frying pan in the area below the stove, I went in my bedroom and played my new 45-rpm records on my old phonograph. One of the records made the phonograph needle skip a little, so I pressed down on the phonograph's arm with the attached needle to straighten out the bad groove. This usually worked but it didn't this time. I tried putting a quarter on the phonograph's arm to keep the needle in the grooves of the record, as I sometimes did. This didn't work either with this record. Therefore, I knew I would have to try to exchange the 45-rpm disk at the record department in Polk Brothers down the street from the music shop where I had my lessons. When I had records from there that didn't work right, they would replace them even though the clerk wasn't happy about doing it for me. I needed a new needle for my phonograph, but it was quicker and easier to take care of skipping records myself. Besides, I was a very impatient person and didn't like to have to wait to correct wrongs. My way of quickly correcting a skipping record caused a hissing sound on the records sometimes, but I wasn't that picky a listener. I was happy just to hear music, even when the sound was somewhat distorted by me pushing the needle into the record's groove to keep the needle from skipping across the record.

While I was listening to the records, Brett had come into the room and was playing with one of his toys on the hardwood floor. I didn't even notice that at some point he had climbed into his bed and was laying down and facing the wall with a pillow over his head. After I put the records and phonograph in the closet, I checked to see if Brett was sleeping by moving his pillow a little and putting my hand up to his face. He didn't stir at all, so I hoped he was out for the night. Then I checked under the bed to make sure nobody was there again. It was a habit I thought I'd never be able to break. Before I climbed up to my bunk bed to fall asleep, I turned out the light and got in praying position. I stayed there for quite a while because I needed to wish Jesus a Happy Birthday and thank the Lord for letting Christmas turn out so wonderful for our family once again. I also thanked Him for letting Grandma be more like her old self again as she didn't make people unhappy by talking so much about Grandpa not being there. I was so certain that she would talk about Grandpa's death a lot during Christmas day just as she kept mentioning him on Thanksgiving, about a month ago. But she didn't. I think the biggest difference between Thanksgiving and today was that Grandma was tired in her bedroom much of the day. When she was out with everyone else, she was busy. She loved to be busy, no matter what the chore was. I thought the best way Grandma could be happy in the future would be if she stayed busy. It would probably be impossible for her to keep herself as busy as she was when she was out of her bedroom to host Christmas activities, but there might be a way for her to keep busy doing other things from now on. Seeing Grandma acting better on Christmas was probably the best gift I'd received. And I needed to let the Lord hear my appreciation for that. After all, I assumed that He is the only one who could give gifts like that.

Chapter Sixteen: New Year's Eve

Two days after Christmas, Murph came over around ten o'clock in the morning. Mom invited him in, and he watched television with me for a while. Then, I showed him everything I got for Christmas. He thought my little frying pan was funny. Beyond it being weird that a ten-year-old got it for a present, it looked funny because most people, like me, would have never seen such a tiny frying pan. He said he didn't like to cook, but he thought it was neat that I knew how. When we were having hot chocolate topped with marshmallows with Mom in the kitchen, he said, "I came over to tell you that we're moving to Chicago tomorrow because my dad starts working at his new job next week." I didn't want to hear it. Not knowing what to say or do, I just stared down at the melting marshmallows in my mug. Breaking the silence, Mom said, "We're going to miss you, Murph. Scott talks about how good a friend you are and how much he enjoys doing things with you."

Uncharacteristic of my shyness, I shook my head in agreement and said, "Yeah, it's going to be different without you around." He said with a bit of a laugh, "Well, you've still got Ray to hang with." Then he got serious and said, "I've got to start making friends all over again." He continued, "And I've got to start all over at a new school again. My mom doesn't even know which school I'll be going to yet. She said I'll probably be going to a Catholic school if there is one near our house. She doesn't want me travelling far on a bus in Chicago, though. Really wish I didn't have to move." Mom said something that I've been finding out is very true when she said, "Sometimes the things we worry about most end up being good experiences. I'm sure everything will turn out just fine for you. Your mom and dad will see to it."

After we made the Chef Boyardee pizza I got for Christmas and ate it, I told Mom that I was going to walk to Murph's house with him. "Don't stay too long, though," she instructed, "His mom won't need company while she's in the middle of packing." Then she said, "And I need to run downtown to get some things. Sue is over at Donna's house, so I will need to take you and Brett with me." I didn't mind that because Dad was at work and not home to take us downtown in the car. That meant we would be taking the bus downtown. Mom didn't drive and I liked going on bus rides to town with her. Mom also said that it was going to get up to about 40 degrees again that afternoon which would be good for going out. As Murph and I walked to his house, he promised to write and send his new address. He also said that he would ask his parents to bring him back sometime to see me. I was hoping his parents had made good friends in Joliet, too, so that they would come back with him occasionally. Time would tell. I knew that I probably wouldn't be going up to Chicago to visit him at his new house because my family either stayed in the Joliet area or took real long vacations during the summer, which started out by heading to the east. Dad only took us to Chicago once in a great while. As close to the big city as we lived, we hardly ever went there.

When we arrived at Murph's, I saw that Mom was right. Their house was not the place to be. There were cardboard boxes stacked from the floor to the ceiling along the living room walls. Lots of them had the word fragile written across them in big red letters. With that warning, I didn't want to touch anything and thought getting out of there before long might be a good idea. But, to make brief conversation with Murph's mom, I asked her if she was finished packing yet. She took us into the kitchen where there were opened boxes awaiting more items before they would be sealed. There were many papers spread out across the kitchen table, too. She pointed at the boxes and the cluttered table and said, "I don't know how I'm going to finish all this before the movers get here tomorrow morning, but I'll have to somehow." I asked her if she had other chores she needed to do before tomorrow. She said, "I should call the electric company, the telephone company, and the post office again just to make sure they stop service. The big thing is the mail. I need them to be sure to forward the mail. None of these things are difficult to do but they do take time." I thought to ask her what their new address would be, but then I didn't because that might give

Murph a reason to not write to me right away. Naturally, I wanted him to write.

I told Mrs. Murphy, "All of this could be avoided if you guys just stayed here." She stopped what she had started doing at the kitchen table, looked at me and said, "How I wish we could stay, Scott." I meant to make her feel good about me not wanting them to go, but her tone of voice made me feel like I'd made her sad instead. Remembering that I had to get home to go downtown with Mom and Brett, I turned to Murph and said, "Don't forget to write." He asked, "What's your mailing address again?" His Mom grabbed a piece of paper and a pencil and handed it to Murph. I said, "2500 North Raynor Avenue," and he wrote it down. Even though he knew the city and state, I said it anyway by saying, "And of course, it's Joliet, Illinois." His mom gave me a big hug and then Murph shook my hand long and hard. Then I left.

I tried to replace my disappointment of his leaving with the pleasant thought that he had spent his last day in town visiting me. Nevertheless, the realization that I might never see him again started setting in. Once again, while I knew that Chicago wasn't very far away by car, Dad very rarely drove there. As far as I could tell, the families who had moved away from our town in the past never came back. It seems that when people leave our town, they're gone for good but yet they're never forgotten. I wondered if they ever thought about us. Though I had only known Murph a couple of months, I knew I would never ever forget him.

This first half of my fifth grade school year was a very important time in my life. I was growing up. Though I was so incredibly busy, I knew in the back of my mind that I was changing a lot during this time. I enjoyed many of the responsibilities I was taking on with my activities, in and out of school. The sense that I was more mature than I had been was from knowing Murph. I was finding that people with whom I spend good times or important times are special, regardless of the length of time I am able to be with them.

After an enjoyable walk to the distant bus stop with Mom and Brett, I really enjoyed looking out the window of the bus as we circled around parts of town that Dad rarely drove through. It was a long ride because the bus had to make so many stops in so many far away neighborhoods before we got to the center of downtown where we got off. Though Brett didn't like it, he constantly had to hold Mom's hand while I just made sure I didn't get separated from them. Yet, if I did get separated from them, I knew my address and I had enough change on me to get back home if I would have gotten lost. Mom and Brett went shopping upstairs in the huge department store and I promised to stay in the record department until they would come to get me. Since I had too much time there, I started looking at the sheet music and read the music and words of the popular songs that they were selling. That sheet music was expensive. One song on paper cost several dollars, which was much more than a 45-rpm recording of the song. I let the melodies run through my mind as I read. When Mom came, she treated all three of us to black cows. I have always loved black cows. They were simple to make as they were just two scoops of vanilla ice cream in a big frosted glass with root beer poured into the glass. Thankfully, Brett couldn't finish his. After I finished mine, I acted like I was doing him a favor by finishing his, too. On the way out of the store, I saw some transistor radio batteries and asked Mom to pick up a couple more. She checked the amount of money she had in her purse and said, "All right. I can do that." The ride home was quite a bit shorter because our neighborhood was one of the first places the bus went after leaving downtown and heading north. There was hardly anybody on the bus but us, and the bus driver asked Mom where we live. After she told him, he went a couple blocks out of his way to drop us off closer to our house than he was supposed to do. Mom told Brett and me to thank the bus driver for saving us time and steps.

As Mom started dinner in the kitchen and Brett went out in the front yard to play with a couple of the neighborhood boys who were about his age, I spent the better part of the remainder of the afternoon in my room. I listened to my transistor radio for a long while and then played some records on my phonograph. I played disc jockey by talking like a radio announcer while I was taking one record off the turntable and putting another one on. It helped me escape from thinking about my days ahead without Murph. Then I forced myself to find some comfort in the fact that I still had Chuck for a friend. There was also hope that Ray would be more likable than he had been in recent times. Hopefully, he would act more like he used to act before he introduced me to Murph. If the old Ray were to return, in spite of himself, I'd want to hang around with him again. However, if he was still in a constant bad mood and saying things that made me feel bad, I'd be better off not seeing him outside of school. If he were to continue acting like a jealous jerk, just because I wouldn't let him be my only friend, I really wouldn't want to spend so much time with him again. I didn't want him to be my only friend without me comfortably having the option of having other friends, too. He was what is referred to as possessive, and I wouldn't allow myself to be possessed.

As I was counting the dwindling days of vacation left and trying not to think about having to go back to school or thinking about Murph being gone, I took an afternoon walk. Midafternoon, the temperature was hovering around 40 degrees which I thought was nice for this time of year. Without much thought, I found myself headed the way I always walked in recent times to go to Murph's house. When I got to the corner where I would have turned to go to his house previously, I couldn't even look down that street. I didn't want to look, thinking it would make me sadder than I was already. Besides, I would have to train myself to quit thinking of that street as Murph's street now that it wasn't his street anymore. With that thought, I kept walking straight ahead. I turned at corners and walked down streets I hadn't walked down recently and eventually found myself within a block of Ray's house. I thought it might be as good a time as any to stop in on him and see how his Christmas was. I could also see if he was in a better mood than he had been in recently. When I knocked on the door, he answered and told me to come down in the basement to see the family's Christmas present to themselves. It was a pool table as big as Murph's. We spent an hour playing eight ball. Though his rules of the game were different from what Murph had at his house, I didn't question Ray's way of playing. If I had started saying that Murph says you're supposed to play this way or that way, he'd just get jealous of me for being friends with Murph again. It was Ray's house and his pool table. Therefore, I just learned his rules and played by his rules. This time, thankfully, it was fun being with Ray again. After a couple of games, I told him I had to be home by five o'clock when my dad would get home from work.

I made it home just in time for dinner. The main course was fish sticks, which meant I didn't eat much at that meal. Except for me, everybody in the family seemed to love fish sticks. I didn't like the taste of the little things. In the past, I put gobs of tartar sauce or cheese on them to drown out the taste of the fish. However, Mom would tell me not to use so much tartar sauce and cheese on them. Maybe she was afraid that I'd use them all up. So, instead of eating the nasty fish, I grabbed as many tater tots as I could so I could try to fill up on them. I really liked those kinds of potatoes, which I would dip in both ketchup and mustard. Incidentally, I liked the story behind the tater tots, too. As the story goes, a potato company, Ore-Ida, decided not to throw away the leftover portions of potatoes that remained after they had cut up their potatoes. Instead, they took the scraps of the potatoes, added seasoning to it and squashed them into little tater tots. I thought it was smart of the company to not waste the leftover potato pieces by throwing them away like they were garbage. Instead, they made them tasty and made money off their garbage. Another thing I liked was that I was older than tater tots, which hadn't even been around for a decade. I liked them more than baked potatoes, mashed potatoes, or French fries, as long as there was ketchup and mustard in the house.

On the afternoon of New Year's Eve, I walked all the way over to Chuck's house even though it was colder outside than it had been on recent afternoons. As per usual, Chuck and his siblings were home alone. Even his little brother was there this time. Whatever Chuck's mom had planned for the big night, New Year's Eve, it didn't include her kids because he said she probably wouldn't be back until after midnight. He wanted me to stay late in his house to do stuff because the temperatures were forecast to be very cold. However, I told him that I'd have to head home in an hour when my dad would be coming home from work. I had to get home because my family always did things together on New Year's Eve. In fact, our family spent all special days together.

Seeing Chuck and his brothers and sister planning on a night at home alone without an adult was foreign to me. Chuck's sister Diane gave me some store-bought candy and cookies, which his Mom apparently bought for her kids to eat at their New Year's Eve celebration without her. I didn't think I ate very much, but Chuck teased me for eating too much too fast. But what else could I have done? She put the stuff in front of me so I'd eat it, right? Even though it was cold out, Chuck wanted to run around the outside of the house just once before it would turn too cold to go out at all. On top of the sore stomach from eating the cheap junk food Diane gave me, I laughed with Chuck until my stomach even hurt more. I usually laughed a lot when I was acting silly with him. Either my eyes were watering from laughing so much or maybe it was my reaction to the cold wind slapping my face.

Though I wanted to stay and have more fun, I could feel tears freezing on my face. After going back in his house to warm up a little bit, I grabbed another cookie and headed home. Since it was about to get dark and the coldest weather would start setting in when it would get dark, I ran part of the way home. For a kid my size, I could run pretty fast when I needed to do so. However, the faster I ran, the deeper I had to breathe. The deeper I breathed, the more my lungs hurt from the cold air. So I decided to do a slow jog most of the way home and ended up getting home just as it had gotten completely dark outside. Except for excused times like Halloween evening or late winter afternoons when I'd be walking home from basketball practice, the rule at our house was that I had to be home by the time the light above the street corner near our house would come on. Being the dead of winter, it got dark awfully early that day. But even though it was just getting dark, the light hadn't come on yet.

When I walked in the kitchen, Mom had already started cooking our traditional New Year's Eve meal, which always included great-tasting Italian sausage in tomato sauce as well as cheese and sausage pizza. From the boiled potatoes on the stove, I knew we were going to be treated to her fantastic potato salad, too. We would also be drinking my favorite pop, Dad's Root Beer. My dad's brother introduced it to us kids a couple of years ago at his house and it had been my favorite soda pop ever since. If we weren't too full, we'd pour the root beer over vanilla ice cream to make a black cow. I preferred my black cows real dark. So, if we had chocolate ice cream in the freezer, I'd get creative and make mine with chocolate ice cream.

After stopping in the bathroom to blow my nose, which had run during my journey home from Chuck's house, I moved the bathroom window's curtain to look outside to see if the streetlight had come on yet. It was on. This meant that, by our house rules, I had gotten home no less than a couple of minutes before I would have been subjected to a lecture from Mom. But maybe, on this late New Year's Eve afternoon, she would have been too busy to notice what was going on outside.

Every New Year's Eve, we also went to a movie at the theater across town. I don't remember much about the movies they picked because I usually didn't care for my parents' choices. This New Year's Eve was no exception. They took us to see *The Alamo*. Dad, in particular, must have been responsible for this one because he's the one who liked westerns, especially westerns starring John Wayne. In this movie, Wayne played the character of Davy Crockett. Brett and I spent lots of time in the lobby until intermission. That was when I saw my fourth-grade teacher Mrs. Lindsay, who was smoking a cigarette, drinking a bottle of Coca-Cola, and eating a chocolate Hershey's candy bar. She was a good-sized woman. I couldn't help but stare at first. I'd never seen her eat, drink, or smoke before. Well, I knew she must have eaten and have drunk before, but I never knew she smoked. What I found unusual was that she was doing all three things at once, which I had never seen anyone do before. Maybe she was in a hurry to get back into the theater to see the movie. Before she might look at me again and possibly recognize me, I grabbed Brett by the arm and went back to our seats inside the theater. I decided I'd stay with Mom, Dad, and Sue just so I wouldn't see Mrs. Lindsay again. Shy people like me don't like to see their teachers in public. It was very late before we finally headed home from the theater because that movie lasted over two-and-a-half hours. Beyond the long length of the movie, there was an intermission, which added more time before the movie ended.

On the way home from the movie, we told one another our New Year's resolutions. Mom initiated this conversation, just as she had other years. She was a strong believer in setting goals for one's self, and then doing all that's possible to achieve the goals. She went first, telling hers. Then, sounding reluctant but playing along, Dad made one up. They probably figured that, by the time they had said theirs, we kids would have had enough time to think of one. Sue said hers next. Then, after not concentrating on anyone else's since I was preoccupied trying to think of my own, it was my turn.

It wasn't that I minded making up New Year's resolutions. In fact, I rather enjoyed doing it after I'd thought one up. But sharing my New Year's resolution with everyone bothered me a little bit. To me, it was a personal thing, and I didn't necessarily appreciate having to go public with it, even if the public was only my family. Beyond them thinking that my resolution might be stupid, sharing my thoughts might reveal something about me that I wanted to keep private. Furthermore, if I announced something like I wanted to lose weight in the next year, I wouldn't want someone nagging me every time I bit into chocolate by saying something about my New Year's resolution going belly up, pun intended. However, I was expected to tell a resolution, so I had to come up with something that I would be willing to share. Needing to borrow more time to think, I said, "It's hard for me to think up just one. There are so many things I want to accomplish." Then I turned to Brett and said, "You go next." He said, "I don't got nothing wrong to do better." While trying to be helpful as well as somewhat humorous, I interjected, "Except to quit murdering the King's English. You should have said that you don't have anything wrong that needs improvement. Honestly Brett, sometimes you talk like you were born in a barn and have been trapped inside since birth." Instead of jumping on Brett for his terribly incorrect way of speaking and for not having a resolution, Sue and my mom jumped on me for causing trouble. "I was just joking," I muttered. It reminded me of the times my mom told me that I often think I'm saying something funny while others aren't thinking I'm humorous at all. Go figure.

Sue firmly said, "Just leave him alone, Scott. He'll learn how to talk better when he gets older." Anyway, my goal, which was to let Brett know that he did have a fault that needed correction, was accomplished. So, I quit talking about Brett's inability to talk without making numerous grammatical errors. Then, surprisingly, Brett did make a New Year's resolution. He said that he'd start washing his hands, without Mom telling him to, before he eats. Unable to resist the opportunity to attempt another joke, I told him he should start washing his face, too. He hit me in the arm as Sue said, "Don't start a fight, Scott." Dad chimed in this time by saying, "Knock it off, Scott." Mom said, "Here we go again." I softly said, "It was supposed to be a joke." Then I just sat there disgusted with myself for what I had allegedly started again, even though I think I had every right to correct his grammar. If nobody corrects him, I figured, how would the kid ever learn how to speak correctly?

To get back on topic, I just blurted out the resolution that was foremost on my mind. I said, "I will treat my friends better in the coming year." Mom turned partially around in her seat and said, "Really? I thought you treated your friends well." "No," I said, "I treated Murph great lately, but I haven't been treating Chuck and especially Ray as well as I could have. I haven't been mean to them, but I've been pretty much ignoring them since I met Murph." After we drove a little further, I said, "From now on, I'm going to spend more time with them, no matter what other friends I find." In a sarcastic tone, Brett said, "Lucky them." I practiced great restraint and didn't respond. Before we pulled in our driveway, Mom said, "Now that the holidays are almost over, you kids should resolve to not eat so much junk." She was probably talking mostly to Brett and me. But it was nice she said it to all of us. This way, I wasn't embarrassed.

At home, we watched television, but my mind was on my New Year's resolutions. I asked Mom, "Can people have more than one resolution?" She said, "Sure! You can have as many as you think you'll keep. But it makes no sense to make a long list of them and then start breaking them right away." At that, I went to my bedroom, got out a piece of paper and a pencil, and laid down on the floor. I listed my New Year's resolutions for the coming year. When I was done writing them down, I wrote numbers in the margin, which showed them listed in order of importance to me. It was an ambitious list, but I felt all of the resolutions were areas in which I needed to improve.

My 1961 New Year's Resolutions

1. I will pray every night. Not only is it the right thing to do, but I want to go to heaven when I die.
2. I will never lie again as I did about smoking because it makes me feel very guilty, because I could get caught in the lie, and because, if I continue lying, I might not get to heaven.
3. I will continue acting less shy because I like myself better when I'm not so shy, and I also think others like me better when I'm not so shy.
4. I will treat my friends better and give every friend some of my time since I feel bad about neglecting Chuck and Ray lately. (This, of course, is the resolution I told the family since it was the first one I thought of when Mom asked for my New Year's resolution. But it isn't the most important. I never would have mentioned number two about lying to

anyone anyway. Apparently, nobody in the family knew I lied about smoking but me.)
5. I will try to make new friends, as I probably should with Tim. I never know who might become another close friend like Murph. If I don't look for new friends, I might not find any. Friends are nice to have and important to have.
6. I will practice my clarinet lesson music and band music at least 30 minutes a day except for the night of my music lesson, nights when the family goes somewhere away from home, or nights when I have too much homework and don't have time to practice. Then I won't feel guilty about the money Dad spends on my lessons anymore.
7. I will ignore people who make fun of me since it makes me unhappy and since Mom says people will eventually leave me alone if I don't react to them.
8. I will quit arguing and fighting with Brett because, by his being younger, he gets me in trouble and wins almost every argument. He makes me look like a bully, even though most of our fights are caused by him being spoiled.
9. I will pay attention more in Sunday school so I'll quit embarrassing myself when the pastor calls on me and I don't know the answer.
10. I will eat less junk because Mom said I should and because I hate being called fat. I hate being fat, too.

Before I ranked the resolutions from one to ten, I had eleven of them written on the front and back of my piece of paper. The one that did not make the top ten said that I would work in school to stay in the "A" row for the rest of the 1960-1961 school year. However, I figured, as proud as I was of being in the "A" row, I would probably do this without making it a New Year's resolution.

After the year 1960, when I'd grown up in so many ways, accepting so many more responsibilities, I was torn between great anticipation and fear of the New Year. However, ready or not, 1961 would arrive shortly. I wanted to stay up until midnight. I managed to do it some other New Year's Eves and knew I'd be able to do it again. Staying up late was never a problem for me when I was excited about something. As I got up from the bedroom floor, I put my list of New Year's resolutions behind the music in my music folder. Mom came in my room to turn down Brett's sheets as Dad carried the little guy in. He was sound asleep in Dad's arms. Mom whispered, "Join us in the living room so I can turn the light off and not wake him." I was pleased that she suggested that I join them rather than tell me to go to bed, too. They must have wanted to stay up a little longer so they'd be awake at midnight.

We watched New Year's celebrations on the television. It was weird watching television this late. I only remember doing it a few times when I'd been sick and couldn't sleep, or a couple other times on New Year's Eve. Dad woke Sue as she slept on the floor in front of the television. Very drowsily, she insisted that she wasn't really sleeping and was going to stay up until midnight. Dad let her continue to lay there, but Mom told her to get to bed because the floor was cold. At this, Sue insisted that she wasn't even tired. "Let her stay, Hon," Dad said, "and we can get her to bed after midnight if that's what she wants." Soon after, Sue was fast asleep on the floor again. Mom got a blanket out of the hallway closet and gently put it over her. I could understand their love for Sue because I loved her just as much.

During the commercials, Mom talked about how much I'd grown up in the past year and how proud she was of all three of us kids. I countered her praise with criticisms of myself. I told her how I could do better if I worked harder and didn't waste so much time enjoying music. Having just finished writing down all of those New Year's resolutions, I guess I was too critical of myself. She disagreed with my self-criticism and continued praising me for doing well in school and in band. She also said that she was proud of how all of us kids behaved around Grandma lately. I knew we behaved well around Grandma most of the time anyway because Grandma would always tell us to behave if we didn't.

Mom explained that Grandma had to cope with more than just Grandpa's death in the past six months. She said that Grandma was sick. I asked, "What do you mean she's sick? How?" As to not wake or worry Sue, probably, Mom began softly whispering, "I don't want you to say anything because I don't want the others to have to worry. But I want you to know so that you'll understand when I tell you and Brett to try to get along better. There's a reason for it. There's a lot going on and I don't need these arguments you two have." Then she continued with the details by saying that Grandma has been going to the hospital for radiation treatments several mornings a week. I didn't know what a radiation treatment was, but it sounded serious. She went on to say that Grandma didn't even realize how sick she was. "How could she not know?" I asked. Mom said, "Faith. Your grandmother has always had very strong faith. It's a wonderful thing to have, especially at a time like this when she needs it. Grandma knows that the people who are going for radiation with her are very ill. She feels very sad for them. But she also believes that she is the one who will be cured." "Will she?" I asked. Mom was hesitant to respond. She then looked away and said, "We'll just have to wait and see, Scott. But I just want you to understand that your grandmother is sick and the fighting between you and Brett don't help matters."

Though I was extremely saddened by what Mom had told me, I shouldn't have been all that surprised. Grandma had always had a lot of energy and kept busy all the time. She rarely sat still. It was obvious that she had less energy recently. Another hint that Grandma wasn't feeling very well was the couple of times I heard her say that she would one day be with Grandpa again. She meant that she would see him in heaven. I figured that she only would be saying that if death were in the back of her mind. I tried to console myself by thinking that Grandma didn't seem like she was sick enough to die real soon because she looked the same as she always did. But then, Grandpa didn't look sick before he died either. I was afraid. I was too afraid to ask Mom how long Grandma had to live. I didn't want to know just then.

Of course, this conversation with Mom also explained why she had acted so differently this school year. Not only had she just lost her father to an unexpected death, but she also had found out that her mother is very ill. I wished I had known all along so that I could have made an extra effort to be good. I sat there thinking how wonderful it was that Grandma had such strong faith to get through a terrible time like this. I hoped my faith would be that strong when I'd need it most. I told Mom and Dad that I really felt bad about Grandma being sick and that I'd try to make things more peaceful at home. Of course, I was thinking about number eight on my New Year's resolutions list, which was to quit fighting and arguing with Brett. Mom said, "I know you love your grandma and will do your best to help out, son." In fact, I was self-consciously starting to think that my argument with Brett tonight was the reason why she was telling me all of this. Maybe it was her way of asking me again to try to get along with my brother better. After this talk, we watched more television, switching the dial in hopes of finding more New Year's celebrations on TV.

At a couple minutes before midnight, Dad opened the door leading to our covered front porch and the door leading to the steps outside our house. He said to Mom and me, "Come here. Even though it's cold out, someone will be out to ring in the New Year. Let's listen." Mom and Dad kissed at midnight. Then she gave me a pat on my shoulder and he brushed the bristly hair on top of my head with the palm of his hand. As they softly sang *Auld Lang Syne*, distant church bells chimed twelve times to tell everyone that it was twelve o'clock, the New Year. Fireworks started popping, distant cars' horns were honking, and people down the street were yelling, "Happy New Year! Happy New Year!" I stepped outside in my stocking feet with Dad and shouted it once after he did it.

So this is what the neighborhood was like at midnight on New Year's Eve. It was the first time Dad had taken me outside to witness it. I had no idea that so many people stayed up and were outside in the cold to welcome the New Year. Soon after, Mom said that we needed to close the door before the mice would sneak in. Staying up late like this, when Sue didn't even make it, made me feel different again. By now, though, I was learning that being different or feeling different wasn't necessarily a bad thing. In fact, I was finding that being different was usually something good.

Dad escorted Sue to her room. She was really out of it, and he practically had to drag her down the hallway to her room. When he came back to the living room, he said, "We're not going to want to get up for church if we don't get some sleep." As Mom turned off the television which was on one of the channels that had a test pattern on the screen after the station's sign-off, and as Dad unplugged the Christmas lights on the Christmas tree, the room went dark except for a little light that shown through the front window from the street light out on the corner. One more time, I softly said, "Happy New Year." Then I went in my bedroom and did my nightly rituals. I checked to make sure Brett was sleeping by putting my hand in front of his face. He didn't stir. Then, of course, I checked under the bed to make sure nobody was there. Naturally, I finally got in praying position and said my routine prayers quickly so I could then pray extra hard for Grandma to be able to live a long, long time yet.

As I laid in bed, not able to sleep, I tried to replace my sad thoughts about Grandma with other thoughts. Since the Christmas vacation was almost over and school would begin in two days, I started mentally challenging myself by silently trying to name the kids in my class, in the order they sat, starting with John in the first desk in the "A" row: John, Ray, Mary, Scott, Sammy, and so on. Somewhere between the "A" row and the "D" row, I was too drowsy to continue. Instead, I drifted off to sleep thinking how I could never quite understand why some kids looked so forward to the first day of school at the end of each vacation.

Chapter Seventeen: Fast Forward

All of this happened a long time ago. Yet I remember the events as if they happened just last week. Looking back to that time, I now realize that 1960 was a great time to be alive. If I had known what was to follow in life, I would have worried less and tried to enjoy myself more as a kid. However, I'm quite sure I was typical in being a kid who didn't realize that being 10 years old is one of the best times of one's life. It's before a person has any real difficult responsibilities and, hopefully, before he has any adult-sized problems. Children who do not enjoy their lives as they are when they are young are missing a lot. They ought to live and enjoy their lives while they can in the present. Though young people probably have no way of knowing it, the part of their lives that they will remember most fondly in the future could very well be the part of their lives they are living now.

So what happened to the characters in this book as time passed beyond 1960? After Murph moved from Crest Hill to Chicago, his friends at Chaney School never heard from him again. Unfortunately, Ray and I ended up going to different high schools and never hung out together again after elementary school, even though we lived so close to one another. I saw his younger sister at a grade school reunion about 25 years after Ray and I had graduated from grade school, and she said he moved not far from Joliet and had a family of his own.

Chuck and I went to the same high school but never had a class together. As things turned out, I was active with band activities and had a part-time job. Chuck was busy with a part-time job, too. Therefore, we didn't have much time to spend together during our high school years. Since high school, we haven't seen each other. I did see his brother Larry and his sister Diane once, some 25 years after we graduated from high school. I didn't recognize Larry as his appearance had changed drastically, but Diane still looked attractively the same. Larry was the one who approached me as he remembered me right away. He said that he was single and that

Diane married her older boyfriend who she was dating when I used to visit their house. When I asked about Chuck, he said that he moved out west and found a job. Larry said Chuck had never come back to the area. Some 25 years after having run into Larry and Diane, members of my high school graduating class were organizing a class reunion. Online, questions were asked as to where certain classmates could be contacted to receive information about the reunion. When I came across Chuck's name as being one of the former students that couldn't be contacted, someone posted that he had passed away. I was – and still am - heartsick.

At these reunions, I saw a lot of familiar faces and many people who I knew by name because they were in the band with me. One of the biggest surprises at a reunion was seeing Bonnie. I recognized her right away as she still had a young-looking face quite similar to the face I knew years ago. She was so nice and appeared to be so glad to see me that I almost felt guilty for initially feeling sick to my stomach when I had seen her there. When I saw her, I had nothing but terrible memories of her treatment of me in school. Anyway, we spoke briefly and she told me that she lived in Joliet for a time after high school, was married and divorced – just once - and then moved to a southern state. She said she used to come back to the area to visit her parents regularly, but she has not been back since both of her parents had passed some years ago.

My immediate family stayed in the Joliet area and remained very connected. I went on to college after high school where a new set of friends replaced the old. Grandma ended up being very unhappy just before she died of cancer in the early 1960s, as one of her children died. One of my mom's two brothers, my uncle, passed away. It was said that he died from a mishap involving prescription medications. Unfortunately, Dad passed away suddenly due to a heart attack while I was in college. That was the most devastating day of my life. Mom got her driver's license, started working as a supervisor in a human resources office, and lived more than 30 years without Dad. Her biggest goal was to see that both Brett and I graduated from college. Thanks to Mom, of all our family members, I was the first to graduate from college and Brett was the second. Mom chose never to remarry again. Sue married, had a couple of children, and got a divorce. Sadly, several years after Mom passed away, Sue was diagnosed with pancreatic cancer and died in her early 60s. Brett married, had six children, and got a divorce. He has always been extremely successful in business and finance throughout his entire adult life. Surprising to many, I'm sure, I didn't enter into a full-time music career. Though I had many part-time jobs involving music through the years, I became an English teacher for more than four decades. I taught English and English as a Second Language, from grades 6 through 14, which is middle school through community college. After retiring from teaching, I have done part-time jobs, primarily as a delivery person. Of course, as one can see by this book, I also became a writer through the years.

About the Author

Scott Paulson is an American English teacher and writer. By attending North Central College in Naperville, Illinois, he earned a bachelor's degree in speech communications accompanied by an Illinois teaching certificate to teach language arts in secondary schools and beyond. After teaching full-time in public schools for over three decades, he taught at community colleges for nearly another decade in the Chicago area. His writings primarily encompass his interests and knowledge of education, teaching, the English and Spanish languages, music, and life. To his publishing credits, he has had many songs, lyric and music, published. A number of them have been recorded. He has also had many magazine, newspaper, and online articles published.

Made in the USA
Middletown, DE
26 May 2025

76116259R00103